Milk, Manna, and Meat

90 Days of Spiritual Nourishment

Dr. Ava S. Harvey, Sr.

Copyright © 2018 Dr. Ava S. Harvey, Sr.

All rights reserved. No part of this book may be used or reproduced by any means, graphic, electronic, or mechanical, including photocopying, recording, taping or by any information storage retrieval system without the written permission of the author except in the case of brief quotations embodied in critical articles and reviews.

WestBow Press books may be ordered through booksellers or by contacting:

WestBow Press
A Division of Thomas Nelson & Zondervan
1663 Liberty Drive
Bloomington, IN 47403
www.westbowpress.com
1 (866) 928-1240

Because of the dynamic nature of the Internet, any web addresses or links contained in this book may have changed since publication and may no longer be valid. The views expressed in this work are solely those of the author and do not necessarily reflect the views of the publisher, and the publisher hereby disclaims any responsibility for them.

This book is a work of non-fiction. Unless otherwise noted, the author and the publisher make no explicit guarantees as to the accuracy of the information contained in this book and in some cases, names of people and places have been altered to protect their privacy.

Any people depicted in stock imagery provided by Getty Images are models, and such images are being used for illustrative purposes only. Certain stock imagery © Getty Images.

Scripture taken from the King James Version of the Bible.

Scripture quotations marked (NIV) are taken from the Holy Bible, New International Version®, NIV®. Copyright © 1973, 1978, 1984, 2011 by Biblica, Inc.™ Used by permission of Zondervan. All rights reserved worldwide. www.zondervan.com The "NIV" and "New International Version" are trademarks registered in the United States Patent and Trademark Office by Biblica, Inc.™

ISBN: 978-1-9736-3210-8 (sc)
ISBN: 978-1-9736-3211-5 (hc)
ISBN: 978-1-9736-3209-2 (e)

Library of Congress Control Number: 2018907375

Print information available on the last page.

WestBow Press rev. date: 07/16/2018

Contents

Acknowledgments ix
Preface xi

Day 1   Little Things Can Cause Big Damage 1
Day 2   Something is Coming 3
Day 3   Is there a Fly in your Ointment? 5
Day 4   If You Can't Help Me, Please Don't Stop Me 7
Day 5   The Tares Go First 9
Day 6   Slow Down 11
Day 7   The Wisdom of the Ant 13
Day 8   Recharging Yourself 15
Day 9   Don't Stay in the Ditch 17
Day 10   Get out of the Ditch 19
Day 11   A Pattern of Good Works 21
Day 12   Pray About It 23
Day 13   Standing Up 25
Day 14   Armed and Dangerous 27
Day 15   Get Dressed 29
Day 16   Wrestling With It 31
Day 17   Be of Good Cheer 33
Day 18   Oh Lord, Deliver Me! 35
Day 19   God's Grace 37
Day 20   He's Enlarging Me Through Distress 39
Day 21   He Heard and Answered 41
Day 22   Be Salt, not Salty! 43
Day 23   Praying Instantly 45
Day 24   Walking With the Wise 47
Day 25   Victory in Vigilance 49

Day 26	But Lord, I'm Trying	51
Day 27	Multiplying and Increasing	53
Day 28	The 24 Hour God	55
Day 29	Humble Beginnings	57
Day 30	In His Hands	59
Day 31	Taking Control of This Year	61
Day 32	Taking Control of Your Mouth	63
Day 33	Taking Control of Your Debt	65
Day 34	Taking Control of Your Income	67
Day 35	Taking Control of Your Savings	69
Day 36	Can You Be Trusted?	71
Day 37	Ants in the Pants	73
Day 38	Staying Motivated	75
Day 39	First Things First	77
Day 40	Are You Having Fun Yet?	79
Day 41	Working For It	81
Day 42	I'm Working On It	83
Day 43	Working While It Is Day	85
Day 44	What's Your Plan?	87
Day 45	What Are Your Expectations?	89
Day 46	Playing By The Rules	91
Day 47	The Next Level	93
Day 48	Next Level Living	95
Day 49	Pray Through It	97
Day 50	Pray With It	99
Day 51	Keep Praying	101
Day 52	Loving and Living in the Light	103
Day 53	The Light Has Come	105
Day 54	Beginning Small	107
Day 55	I Shall Not Want	109
Day 56	Green Pastures	111
Day 57	He Leads Me	113
Day 58	He Restores Me	115
Day 59	The Paths of Righteousness	117
Day 60	Walking through the Valley	119
Day 61	The Valley of the Shadow of Death	121
Day 62	The Valley of the Shadow of Death	123
Day 63	The Valley of the Shadow of Death	125

Day 64	The Rod & Staff	127
Day 65	The Presence of Mine Enemies	129
Day 66	The Prepared Table	131
Day 67	Thou Anointest My Head	133
Day 68	My Cup Runs Over	135
Day 69	For Goodness Sakes	137
Day 70	Lord Have Mercy	139
Day 71	What's Following Me?	141
Day 72	The Days of our Lives	143
Day 73	Take me to Church	145
Day 74	Be Faithful	147
Day 75	Be Committed	149
Day 76	Be Prepared	151
Day 77	Be Thankful	153
Day 78	Be Holy	155
Day 79	Be Glad	157
Day 80	Be Planted	159
Day 81	Be Prosperous	161
Day 82	Be of Good Courage	163
Day 83	Be Made Whole	165
Day 84	Dealing with Disappointment	167
Day 85	Dealing with Frustration	169
Day 86	Dealing with Setbacks	171
Day 87	Dealing with Mistakes	173
Day 88	Perfect in Weakness	175
Day 89	A Life in Progress	177
Day 90	Good Things Are Coming!	179

Acknowledgments

I dedicate this devotional to the God of all creation, the only wise One from which all things exists and to His Son, Jesus Christ, my Lord and life-changer and the precious promise of power and presence, the Holy Spirit. I devote every letter, word, sentence, and readable thought in this work to my loving wife Leslee and my darling children Amari and Ava Jr. To my entire family, friends, and loved ones, thank you for all your prayers, support, and encouragement. Last but not least, tremendous appreciation goes to the greatest church on this side of heaven, Pilgrim Rest Missionary Baptist Church of Brandon, Mississippi. Your unfailing love and support has provided me the space to reach higher in the Lord. I thank God for all of you!

Preface

Becoming a Christian was a life-altering experience for me. I was senior in High School and preparing to transition from the familiarity of family and friends, while also trying to choose which educational direction to pursue. The stress of not knowing what to do and the complication of finding my real identity in Christ were often overwhelming. There were times when I felt ill prepared to face the challenges that came with the naivety of youth and the certainty of change.

As I look back on those days of being a teenaged Christian, there were several people who provided solid advice and helpful encouragement to my faith. Their insightful, timely, and wise counsel helped to strengthen my relationship with God. Milk, Manna, and Meat seeks to do the same for you. It is an easy-to-read ninety-day devotional that offers spiritual nourishment and encouragement for Christians in every stage of development. On each page, I offer compassionate advice and sound lessons from the Bible that can be immediately applied to your life.

Day 1

Little Things Can Cause Big Damage

> Galatians 5:9 A little leaven leaveneth the whole lump.

Leaven in the bible days is the equivalent to yeast in our day. For those who have an appreciation for baking bake bread, you know how important the components of yeast are to your mixture. Without yeast, the bread would not rise and it would essentially look like a big flat piece of pancake. Yeast has agents of bacteria within it that cause the entire loaf to lift when heated. It makes bread puffy and bloated and also changes the taste entirely. The bible compares leaven (yeast) to sin. This is why when the Children of Israel were leaving Egypt God told them to bake "unleavened bread" as part of the Passover meal. Unleavened meant that the bread would be flat but it would also be without the symbolism of sin (leaven/yeast). They were to clean their entire house of all leaven and sweep it totally clean of anything possessing leaven. There are seven Great Feast of Israel and one of them is the Feast of Unleavened Bread; which is actually a memorial of how God brought a mighty deliverance for His people. It doesn't take much leaven to change the make-up of the bread; just a little dab will alter its taste, nature, and appearance. Consequently, it doesn't take much sin to alter our fellowship with God. Paul uses this powerful illustration to convey the meaning to the church at Galatia – "a little leaven leaveneth the whole lump." The idea is that sin causes changes no matter how small we think it may be. So often we are quick to quantify the amount of things we aren't doing sinfully in our flesh, but what about the sins and filthiness of the spirit? What about the hidden thoughts, pride, arrogance, conceit, lust, envy, covetousness, and even a mis-managed mind? See it's not always the big things that cause great harm, it's the little foxes that destroy the vine. We must distance ourselves from sin because sin will ultimately lead to death. Let's start this day off by asking God to clean us from the inside out that we may walk in His ways and please Him. Let's ask Him to remove the leaven that would cause us to be puffed up and bloated in our hearts and minds. If we confess our sins He is faithful and just to forgive us and to cleanse us from all unrighteousness.

Day 2

Something is Coming

> John 16:13 Howbeit when he, the Spirit of truth, is come, he will guide you into all truth: for he shall not speak of himself; but whatsoever he shall hear, that shall he speak: and he will shew you things to come.

The idea of having something to look forward to keeps us hopeful and excited. Whether it's a date on the calendar for a big event, your birthday, or any special occasion that's on the horizon, it's exciting to know it will soon be here. Studies show that people who have an active schedule live much longer than those who do not. Thus it behooves us all to be busy, but not just for the sake of being busy. Our "busyness" should be with a business purpose. If you have not been busy, start today. Today's passage captures the words of Christ. He says the Spirit of Truth (Holy Spirit) has come to guide every believer into more truth. It stands to reason that the revelation of truth is both collective and individual. In other words, His truth is conveyed to each individual believer as he or she receives it. The fact that Jesus says: "He will show you things to come," also suggests that we do not have everything nor do we know everything right now. There is more in store for us. Something is coming! Are you ready? Just like a preview of a movie displays snippets and portions of what's to come, and promoters push an upcoming event; even so does the Spirit of truth. Listen to His leading, follow His voice and walk in expectation of things to come.

Day 3

Is there a Fly in your Ointment?

> Ecclesiastes 10:1 Dead flies cause the ointment of
> the apothecary to send forth a stinking savour.

It's virtually impossible to have a barbecue, cook out or fish fry without the unpleasant appearance of flies. From picnic joys, birthday parties, and softball games to lawn duty, the fly has always been a nuisance. Someone once asked the question; "did Noah take two mosquitoes on the ark, if so; why didn't he just smash them and end our misery?" We can revise the question to ask why didn't he kill the last two flies too? Flies are so irritating. They are attracted to our food and somehow always find a way to get into the house. Countless money is spent each year on flyswatters and unfortunately I never seem to have one when I need it. The passage today reveals to us that when flies get into the ointment of the apothecary; it begins to stink. The apothecary is what we would call a modern day pharmacist. He is the one who prepares medicine for sick people. Literally, the ointment was an oily cream that was applied to the place of infection. When a fly was in the ointment; it meant that something small was contaminating the whole thing. No one in the right mind would anoint his or herself with something that could potentially make them worse instead of better. The flies in your life must be dealt with before they contaminate the very medicine that's designed to heal you.

Day 4

If You Can't Help Me, Please Don't Stop Me

St. Mark 10:48 And many charged him that he should hold his peace: but he cried the more a great deal, Thou Son of David, have mercy on me.

Have you noticed that the banks and reputable lending institutions only loan money to people who don't need it? Isn't it strange that it's easier to find a job when you already have one? And why does the item you just bought go on sale the next day? It goes without saying; when you need something the most, it's usually the most difficult time to get it. In today's passage blind Bartimaues is begging for help by the highway side in the city of Jericho. He already has three strikes against him; he's blind, he's begging, and he's being told to be quiet. The man needs help but it's hard to get it with these odds against him. The crowd is telling him to hush! We have no way of knowing how many people were in the crowd; but he had to cry louder than the crowd to get Jesus' attention. Why would all these people try to stop a blind man from receiving his sight? Why would anyone prevent a beggar from getting help? It seems cruel and harsh to think of people telling a person with a natural human defect to move out of the way but it happens all the time. They can't help him;

but they're actively preventing him from receiving help! Have you ever been in a situation where someone couldn't help you but then they also tried to stop you from getting help? It's called blocking! Thankfully, Jesus heard him over the crowd. Don't be afraid to cry louder and go around the blocks to get what you need. There are 3 Blocks you need to get around: 1) The Block of Discouragement 2) The Block of Disappointment and 3) The Block of Distress.

Day 5

The Tares Go First

> Matthew 13:30 Let both grow together until the harvest: and in the time of harvest I will say to the reapers, Gather ye together first the tares, and bind them in bundles to burn them: but gather the wheat into my barn.

Most believers are waiting on the manifestation of their harvest. Over the years, they've planted seeds of faith financially, spiritually, and physically; with hopes that soon there would be a great return on that investment. Needless to say, receiving a spiritual harvest isn't always as predictable as it may be in the natural process. Our Spiritual harvest can be delayed by our spiritual development or lack thereof and the personal and practical application of many Biblical truths in our lives. There are even people who are expecting a miraculous harvest without ever even sowing any seeds at all. We should be aware that when we sow in faith, we must also maintain that faith throughout the duration of the entire process. When the enemy sows tares among your wheat; remain faithful. When others ask questions about the tares in your field; remain faithful. When you're forced to sit back and do nothing about the tares that are growing beside your wheat; remain faithful. When you've done all you know to do; and your field is now full of tares and wheat; remain faithful. Why? Because when the harvest finally comes, the tares are removed first. I've thought long and hard as to why the owner harvested the tares before the wheat and one main reason stood above all others. He wanted to see his field fully mature with wheat before he harvested any of it. The owner sowed only good seeds but up until this point; he'd not seen his field without tares being mixed among the wheat. God is so good that he'll allow the removal of the tares first in order for us to see how beautiful our field really is and to confirm that our labor was not in vain.

Day 6

Slow Down

> Psalms 102:24 I said, O my God, take me not away in the midst of my days: thy years are throughout all generations.

Most of us are always in a hurry. We walk fast, talk fast, eat fast, and just do everything thing fast. We rush, we move quickly, we hurry to work, we hurry to school, we drive fast and yes we even worship fast. It's time to slow down. Think of all the things we've missed because we just didn't have time to enjoy them. Time is our most precious commodity on earth and how we use it determines a great deal of our livelihood. We must make the most of every opportunity because we won't always have them. Just because things are like they are now, doesn't mean that they'll always be that way. For many, the ages of 70 or 80 years old, sounds like a long way away. Yet in reality it's only a matter of perception. It's not as far off as we think. At one point in life we probably wished we were older. Have you ever wished you were a teenager when you were eight years old? Or out of High School when you were a freshman? Or out of College when you were a junior? Or twenty-one when you were eighteen? We wished we were older because we wanted to experience what came with that age. But somewhere in life we stopped wishing to go up in age and started reminiscing on when we were younger. In some cases, we even wished we could go back to those early days of life and redo some things. Well, time doesn't reverse. This is why we need to slow down. If you're anything like me; when you see these young people trying to grow up so fast; you wish you could get them to see that life is too short to rush it away. We can manage time, enjoy time, and spend time wisely; but we can't make it stop. Look at how much time we've wasted by doing absolutely nothing or going after things that have no long-term value at all. We can all do better with our use of time and we can also slow down enough to appreciate every opportunity. Slowing down doesn't mean we can't get things done expediently; but it does mean we can cherish and enjoy them while we're doing them.

Day 7

The Wisdom of the Ant

Proverbs 6:6 Go to the ant, thou sluggard;
consider her ways, and be wise:

Wisdom can be found in some of the most unusual places. All we need to do is be attentive to the environment around us and we'll see firsthand just how much wisdom is in the basic things of life. Every animal and all insects have natural instincts that guide, protect, and carry them throughout the course of their lifecycles. Without these instincts, they would be unable to perform the simple task that they do each day. If bees did not gather nectar from flowers to make honey, we'd soon see the complete demise of all flowers. The act of gathering nectar serves to pollinate flowers and thereby reproduce more flowers continuously. If buzzards did not clear the streets and roads of all dead animals our highways would be littered with all kinds of creatures that failed to cross the roads. Believe it or not, ants are involved in both of these processes too. When pollen has fallen, ants are instrumental in moving it to flowers by transverse and they also participate in the consumption of dead animals. Ants are everywhere. There are over 22,000 species of ants with 12,500 of them being classified. It's interesting that ants can survive the most hostile environments in the world and thrive in spite of being considered a pest. By observing the wisdom of the ant we can closely identify ourselves with the various types. Some of us are like the Fire Ant. The Fire Ant is one of the most aggressive ants of all types. Their sting is terribly awful to experience and frustrating to anyone who has been bitten by one. Some people are the same as Fire ants. They have aggressive personalities that push people away and when they sting the affects are horrible. They sting with their lies, betrayal, and harmful words. There's another ant called the Carpenter Ant. The Carpenter Ant gets his name because they build their nests in wood. They do not eat the wood, but they remove it to establish a home. Because they are removing the wood, they are conversely making their home weaker and they'll soon have to move again. Some people have the personality of Carpenter Ants too. They are making decisions that they think are for their good; but they're decisions are actually weakening their lives and homes. Ironically, the Carpenter Ant isn't constructing anything; it's actually destroying it. Then there's the Worker Ant. The Worker Ant is one that simply works. He goes to work every day and gets the job done. While others are focused on everything other than work, this ant has a record of accomplishment. Some people are like the Worker Ant. They mind their own business and get their work done. The passage instructs us to consider the ant. Which one are you?

Day 8

Recharging Yourself

> Jude 20 But ye, beloved, building up yourselves on
> your most holy faith, praying in the Holy Ghost,

If you have a cell-phone, laptop, or any type of mobile electronic device you know the importance of having a charger. Many of the video games that our children enjoy also come with mobile chargers. We have them in our cars, in our offices, at home, and any place that we can get power (juice) from. I've watched people search for outlet plugs at airports so that they could "recharge" prior to departing on a flight. I've also seen people requesting to be seated near an outlet at a restaurant so that they can build up their battery. Each night most of us plug our cell phones up and let them remain plugged in all night long so that we'll have their full usage on the next day. If we fail to let them charge, we'll soon be wishing we had. In fact, sometimes even when our devices are charged we still connect them to the chargers in our vehicles to ensure that we're fully juiced. The importance of being charged up cannot be understated. Even our cars have alternators that keep our batteries charged. No matter how new our car battery may be, if we don't have a functioning alternator we'll soon be stranded in the streets. When it comes to the things of the Lord, we also need to recharge our batteries. Jude teaches us to build up ourselves by plugging into the outlet of faith and praying in the Holy Spirit. We have several factors that contribute to the loss of power. Satan is out to steal, kill, and destroy; thus the need to remain powerful (charged up) is not an option but a necessity. I encourage you not to leave home without praying for power to face the challenges of that day but also you'll need to take a charger with you too. Why not pray (charge up) in the car on your way to school, work, or throughout your day? It would be great to also charge up when you get to your destination. Whether you're in an airport, restaurant, or on a college campus, continue to charge. We have what we need to make it; but unless we're charged we won't be able to utilize what we have. If you're like me, you've been in situation where you needed your cell-phone but for whatever reason, it was not charged. Maybe it was through neglect or you simply failed to bring your charger with you; but your phone went dead. A dead phone can't make or receive calls, text, or email updates. Could it be that we're not receiving what God is trying to reveal to us because our life is uncharged. Maybe we're charging up in the morning, but by noon we're already blinking and about to expire. Be prepared to charge yourself throughout the day. We don't have to remain plugged in all the time; but we do need to plug in from time to time.

Day 9

Don't Stay in the Ditch

> Luke 6:39 And he spake a parable unto them, Can the blind lead the blind? shall they not both fall into the ditch?

Today's passage is one the most famous parables that Jesus ever taught. Almost anyone with any depth of scripture knowledge knows or has heard this parable preached, taught and explained. Usually the emphasis is placed on the need to be aware of who you're following. Obviously, if we follow someone who doesn't know where they're going; we'll end up exactly where they are. The symbolism of "the blind leading the blind," suggest that both people are totally clueless as to where they should be going. One person is a follower and the other is a leader. Imagine for a moment the unfortunate reality that hundreds of thousands of people are following blind leaders. Most of us would be sympathetic to a blind follower; but hardly anyone has sympathy for a blind leader. Of course, I'm not referring to natural blindness but rather spiritual blindness. However, the similarities are overwhelming. Blindness is a very serious condition. It can occur in all kinds of ways. Some people are born blind while others develop blindness through diseases and sickness. There are also thousands of people who become blind accidentally through mishaps, mistakes, and negligence of themselves or others. The blind simply cannot lead the blind, either physically or spiritually. Yet the emphasis for our passage is not so much about the blindness but we're looking at the place that it leads to – the ditch. You don't have to stay in the ditch. While it is important to know how you got there it's more important to know how you're going to get out. The ditch can be more than just a physically low place; it can also be an emotionally or spiritually low. When we are low we are usually in despair, ill, in trouble, challenged, or in hardships. Each one of these words symbolizes what the DITCH is. D=despair I=ill T=trouble C=challenged H=hardships. The ditch can be a lonely place, but it's usually filled with people who have been led there by blind leaders. Unfortunately, everybody isn't ready to come out of the ditch. There are many who are comfortable with "ditch-living." They have lowered their expectations and lost hope that their lives can change for the better. Are you one of them? If you want to get out of the ditch, you can but it's up to you. If nobody gives you a helping hand, help yourself. If nobody gives you a leg up, climb up. I nobody gives you an opportunity, create your own.

Day 10

Get out of the Ditch

> Luke 6:39 And he spake a parable unto them, Can the blind lead the blind? shall they not both fall into the ditch?

When I think of ditches my mind automatically goes to roadside ditches that are used to funnel water. As a young child, my friends and I used to play in the ditches. The ditch was a natural place to find interesting things like old Indian arrowheads or coins. One day, we decided to be like the motor cross cyclist superstar Evel Knievel, the motorcycle daredevil of the 60's and 70's. He was once rumored to have jumped the Grand Canyon but he never actually did. In fact, many of his major stunts and jumps were unsuccessful; but his popularity was soaring because he kept making outrageous attempts to jump things. Somehow on that day we felt compelled to take our pedal-driven bicycles down the hill to jump a ditch with Evel Knievel on our minds. The feat was very doable because the ditch was only about four feet wide and three feet deep. The only problem any of us would encounter was if we didn't have enough speed for our momentum to carry us over the ditch. Once we got to the edge of the ditch, all we'd have to do was lift our bikes in the air and land safely on the other side. I'm not really sure how I was drafted to go first; but without any fear, doubt, or unbelief; I started my descent down the hill in full speed. Without any hesitation I jumped the ditch and landed smoothly on the other side with no problem. One by one, we all made it over again and again. We jumped the ditch numerous times until one friend decided on his next turn, that he would let go of the handlebars in the air and yell out "Evel Knievel!" Needless to say, neither he nor his bicycle made across the ditch; they both crashed in the middle of the ditch. It was really a blessing that he was not seriously injured. Everyone quickly came to make sure he was ok, (and he was) but soon after we were reassured of his safety – the laughing and mocking started. In protest, he decided he'd stay in the ditch and block anybody else from jumping it. We encouraged him to come out of the ditch, but he was too embarrassed and upset to come out. Most of us aren't in ditches in our lives for the same reason my friend was; but the solution is the same – get out of it. Maybe you're acting like he was acting by trying to prevent others from crossing over the ditch. Or is it possible that you're in the ditch because of your own choices but now you're so embarrassed until you won't come out. If you've fallen in a ditch accidentally or have followed someone you trusted into a ditch; get out of it. Don't wallow in the mud of despair any longer. If you come out of the ditch, you too can cross on over to the other side of blessings like many others are.

Day 11

A Pattern of Good Works

> Titus 2:7 In all things shewing
> thyself a pattern of good works:

Many things require a pattern in order to be made. Clothes, houses, cars, and most of the goods that we purchase require patterns. Patterns are all around us. They exist in nature through natural occurrences and through man-made invention. God is a God of patterns. He spends a great deal of time communicating His pattern for our lives through His Word. He establishes patterns through His laws and both the Old and New Testaments. Patterns are important for all kinds of reasons. First of all, patterns give us a blueprint of what works. There's no need to reinvent the wheel. All we need to do is use what's already present to better our position. Follow the successful patterns of success. Of course everyone doesn't use the same pattern to achieve their goals and there are slight variations along the way; but the basic points of success are similar across the board. Secondly, patterns give us a direction of which to follow. There's really no need to be lost or have no sense of direction for your life. All you have to do is get on the road that others have traveled. Most of the time that road will take you through a college, university, or advanced educational facility. At other times that road may lead us to a path of entrepreneurship, partnership, or to the employment field. Whatever the road that you're traveling, be mindful that you must be willing to work for what you want. Too often people want immediate success and have no idea of how much reflection, energy, time and work is needed to accomplish it. There's really no such thing as an overnight wonder. Even those stars (Actors, Singers, and Athletes) that shine bright for brief periods of time took a path to get there. It takes time to really become successful. When we put in the work, we can expect the reward. In order to establish a pattern of good works; we must make the efforts needed to accomplish it. There are four C's that are a part of the Pattern of Good Works: 1) Commitment – working towards a goal will require tenancy. Accomplishment and achievement are never easy. 2) Calculation – thinking extensively about how to figure things out. We have to assume that there will be roadblocks and obstacles in the way, but we must learn to use our minds to find solutions. 3) Consistency – being able to do the same thing repeatedly. There will be times when we have to do hard things for a long time, but don't get discouraged. Keep being consistent and it will pay off in the long run. 4) Character – we should never let the things we want to do undermine the person we want to be. Building strong character happens when we are shaped into people that reflect a good pattern of works and emit the image of Christ in our lives.

Day 12

Pray About It

> Luke 18:1 And he spake a parable
> unto them to this end, that men ought
> always to pray, and not to faint;

In this Christian walk, there are periods of time when we feel as if we're walking all alone. Some of the most challenging times of our life can be when our faith is being tested to every extreme. When we are trying to remain true in confidence and assured in hope; a real prayer life can make the difference. Prayer can be the compass to help us to navigate the storms of life. Prayer gives us power and grounds us with supernatural strength. You don't have to be an expert to pray; all you need is a sincere heart. We must learn to talk to God just like we talk to one another. Communication does not have to be complicated. God is waiting to hear from us. It's time to pray earnestly because some things we simply can't change by ourselves. God expects us to call upon Him in our times of trouble and receive the help that we need. Prayer is the key and faith unlocks the doors of opportunity but we can never get in unless we pray. The passage confirms that our prayer life is a direct reflection on our lives. In other words we cannot truly live in faith beyond our prayer life. The manner, mechanics, and motivation of our prayers translate into everything else that we do. I'm concerned that the church today has made prayer a cosmetic thing. God hasn't lost His power, but we have lost our sensitivity to God's power. It is a divine privilege to be able to pray. Wishing for things to change or complaining about how bad things are doesn't change anything. Being discouraged, feeling sorry for yourself, or trying to give up won't make your life get better either. The best thing that we can do is pray; especially when we're being tested. Please note that life can hit you with so much at one time until it's impossible for you to manage it all alone. You or maybe someone you love may be under great distress and the situation is spiraling out of your control – just pray. The pressures of life can oppress and depress anyone at any time. Oppression is all of the things that are happening around you and outside of you; but Depression is what is going on within you. Usually oppression can lead to depression if we aren't prayerful. You know you're under pressure and it's time to pray when you find yourself crying and you don't know why. It time to seriously pray when your thoughts escape you, you're tired but you can't stop going, and nobody understands what you're going through even when you try to explain it. In times like these, we need to pray. I'm encouraging each of you to take time out of your schedule today and pray. Don't just pray a minimal prayer because I asked, but honestly and sincerely go before God with a really earnest prayer.

Day 13

Standing Up

> Ephesians 6:11 Put on the whole armour
> of God, that ye may be able to stand
> against the wiles of the devil.

From our earliest stages of human development we learned how to stand. The natural progression began with scooting, crawling, standing, taking steps and finally walking. Yet, the act of standing is one of the most overlooked stages because we are eagerly anticipating and expecting the baby to walk soon. It is easy to see how "standing" is still taken for granted. No one can truly appreciate the blessing it is to be able to stand unless they've lost utility of the lower body. Let's not take for granted the privileges we've been afforded with the use and activity of our limbs. In the physical sense, standing speaks of being physically able to balance oneself in the erect position of posture. It's interesting that the terminology of "standing" is credibly applied in the spiritual tenses too. God views a Christian that is "standing" as being "upright." In other words, he or she is not upside down but rather right side up! We are encouraged to stand up and be counted in God's army but also to take a stand of faith in this wicked world. Today's passage teaches us to put on the whole armor and stand against the wiles of the devil. In order to "stand against," we must first already be in the upright position. To put it another way, we can't stand against anything (especially the wiles of the devil), if we aren't already standing up. Too often unprepared believers want to jump into spiritual warfare and they aren't upright. We simply can't fight in the seated position nor can we join the fight if we haven't already been taking a stand of faith and living upright. If we have been standing we can now stand against the wiles of the enemy ferociously and without fear. We will soon learn that we aren't fighting nor standing alone. Someone else has already been standing against and fighting against the wiles of the enemy long before we joined the fight. The battle isn't yours alone, even though it may appear that way. There are millions of believers who are praying just as much and likely more than you and I are. So when we join the fight, we actually "stand with" others who have like-minded faith and spiritual insight. We want the kingdom of darkness to be limited in its effect, hindered in its efforts, and ultimately destroyed by the works of the kingdom of God. Through the power of agreement we now can "stand for" Jesus as a united body. Here's the summary: Stand up – Stand Against – Stand With – Stand For – and after you've done all you can do – STAND!

Day 14

Armed and Dangerous

> Ephesians 6:11 Put on the whole armour
> of God, that ye may be able to stand
> against the wiles of the devil.

Armor is defined as being a protective covering used to prevent damage from being inflicted to an object, individual, or vehicle through use of direct contact weapons or projectiles usually during combat. The word armor has its roots in the word "arms" which is the combination of the equipment and gear needed to fight. The human body is not designed to sustain substantial injuries by weapons. Even though our skin is a protective covering over our entire body, it isn't able to handle hard hits from projectiles, arrows, and bullets. Because we are frail there was and is a need to put on something else to cover us; thus man invented armor. When we think about armor, most people tend to only focus on metal-plated armor used by knights but armor can be made out of all kinds of materials. The first armor was probably made of out of wood bark, dry animal skins, or clay. Of course today, armor has evolved tremendously to include bulletproof material and radar reflective metals. Yet the basic need and purpose for all armor is the same thing as it has always been – protection. God tells us to put on the whole armor because He knows we will need protection. We have a real enemy that has intentions to do us much harm. The armor belongs to God but it's available to us. Unfortunately, every believer doesn't put on the whole armor. Some believers chose to steer totally away from the whole idea of spiritual warfare. But whether we are fighting back or not, the devil is fighting us. He's not going to be peaceful towards us and not attack us because we're not interested in fighting. No, he is always fighting. In fact, he is fighting us in places we probably aren't aware of yet. He also doesn't fight fair, he doesn't care if you like Jesus, he doesn't mind you coming to church and he doesn't mind you carrying a Bible or doing anything religious. He is still fighting you. If you don't have on the whole armor, you're sustaining hard hits that will eventually take you out. It's just a matter of time before you will become discouraged, distressed and depressed. The key to staying in the fight is to put on the whole armor of God for protection. Anything that is not protected is in danger of being injured, dismembered, or destroyed completely. You are in danger right now if you don't have this armor on. In order to put it on, we must come to God and get fitted with the right sizes. There's also an under armor that must be put on too; and it's called the "garment of praise." You can put on your garment of praise with thanksgiving and worship right now! So let's get dressed and fight back today!

Day 15

Get Dressed

> Ephesians 6:11 Put on the whole armour
> of God, that ye may be able to stand
> against the wiles of the devil.

The whole of anything is the full quantity, amount, extent, number, and content of that thing. It contains all the elements and is undivided in its essence. After looking at the word "whole," its meaning can be applied to all kinds of variations of life itself. A person is considered whole when they are free from wounds and injury. A pie is considered whole if no slices have been deducted. A loaf of bread is whole if all of the slices remain in place. The whole of anything is all of it in its entirety. The passage tells us to put on the whole armor of God. Essentially we are to put on the full amount of the entire armor. By putting everything on, we don't run the risk of being undressed and missing specific pieces. We need it all! Every morning, as we prepare to face our days we get dressed. A large part of what we intend to do that day helps to determine how we should dress. If you have a very simple day (like a Saturday), which doesn't include getting out of the house much, you probably aren't going to put on a suit or tie. If you are headed to work this morning, you are dressing for the office or putting on the appropriate attire for your field of employment. Students get dressed for classes and sometimes for whatever else they have to do on the campus that day. We normally dress according to what we have to do for that entire day but occasionally we have to come home and change clothes for another event or place we have to go on the very same day. I'm sure there are people on this email list who have changed clothes several times throughout any given day for the various tasks you have to accomplish. Some people even take a change of clothes with them to one place and change on their way to another. Many professionals are identified by what they wear each day; Police officers, Doctors, Dentist, Firemen, and even Fast Food Workers are easily known by their uniforms. But when it comes to the armor of God, we don't change out like we do other garments. We need to remain dressed in the whole armor all the time. Why? Because the moment you take something off, the enemy will hit that spot. We aren't wearing the armor for decoration or style; but rather we are wearing it for our spiritual survival. The quickest way to get injured, wounded, and knocked out of the fight is to be undressed. We can't buy the armor of God at outlet or retail stores. It can only be found in prayer. Put on the whole armor of God in its entirety and cover yourself first. After you have covered yourself, you can use the shield to help to cover others. The battle is raging and it's time to fight back.

Day 16

Wrestling With It

> Ephesians 6:12 For we wrestle not against flesh and blood, but against principalities, against powers, against the rulers of the darkness of this world, against spiritual wickedness in high places.

Wrestling is one of the earliest forms of civil sporting entertainment. The coliseums of Rome, which modeled the amphitheaters of many African cultures, were constructed to be arenas for public entertainment. Within those amphitheaters, champion wrestlers would come from all over the Roman Empire to exhibit their skills. These men would wrestle until the death and ultimately the last man standing was the winner. In modern times, wrestling has become a multi-million dollar entertainment industry. No one is wrestling to the death anymore, in fact; they aren't even seriously wrestling. Their moves are contrived and predictable and the hits, kicks, and matches are all choreographed. Believers are in a wrestling match too. We are wrestling against four types of spiritual entities (Principalities, Powers, Rulers of Darkness, and Spiritual Wickedness). Our matches aren't fake nor for entertainment but we are grappling for our spiritual survival. Our wrestling matches are primarily being held in our minds. The enemy seeks desperately to win the match in our minds by bombarding us with his thoughts. Most people aren't aware that thoughts can enter into our minds by more than one way. God can give us thoughts, Satan can give us thoughts, people can give us thoughts, the world can give us thoughts and we can think our own thoughts. Sometimes it's difficult to tell where all of these thoughts are coming from and Satan often disguises the thoughts he wants us to think by making them appear to be from God. The scriptures tell us that Satan can appear to be an angel of light. In other words, he looks like he's out to do good but his motivation hasn't changed – destroy. Any thought that has us worried, fearful, or doubting whether the Lord will be faithful to His promise is not of God. It behooves us to be mindful that things aren't always what they look like nor is every voice from God. Thus we are taught to cast down imaginations and every high thing that exalts itself against the knowledge of God and to bring every thought into captivity. To put it another way, we are to arrest, test, and decide if what we're thinking is of God (edifying) or not. This is the real wrestling match. It's the continual engagement of the utility of the mind. If we wrestle the enemy with the Word in our minds we can win, but if we're trying to do it on our own; the battle is already lost. It's time to wrestle with it and get some control over the thoughts running through your mind.

Day 17

Be of Good Cheer

> John 16:33 These things I have spoken unto you, that in me ye might have peace. In the world ye shall have tribulation: but be of good cheer; I have overcome the world.

Cheer up! It's another day that the Lord has blessed you to see. Perhaps this week has been a tough one. Maybe this month or year has been long and very taxing but you should rejoice and be of good cheer because the Lord has remained faithful to you through it. There's nothing Christ-like in having a gloomy, pessimistic, and unappealing attitude for a believer. We honor God when we show cheerfulness. To be of good cheer is to be happy. In fact it is an imperative commandment to be happy. In other words we don't have a choice in the matter nor is it our decision. It's not up to us nor is it determined by our circumstances whether or not we should be happy. Someone once wrote, "happiness is contingent upon the happenings of our lives;" but everything that's happening is not always visible. We can be happy even when things don't look like they are getting better for us. We can rejoice in spite of our situations and conditions. Joy is a natural part of our lives. I find it disappointing to see so many Christians walking around with their heads hanging down. God has been too good to us to live in defeat.

We have the victory in the name of Jesus – believe it! In today's passage, Jesus tells the reader that the world will create a climate of contention for believers. In this world, we will have tribulations, trials, test, and challenges. Jesus did not deny the obvious truth about the hardships that await us. Yet within the same breath He tells us to stay happy. In other words, don't let anything steal your joy. We can safely conclude that anything that happens to us can be used to praise God. Yes, even bad things can have good things to come out of them. The Bible doesn't teach us to rejoice "about" everything; but it says to give thanks "in" everything. This is the definition of cheer! When we learn how to be thankful and worship God in tribulations; we've developed the right attitude. Why be of good cheer? One reason is because Jesus Christ has already overcome the world. He conquered the world for us through His life, death and resurrection. He is telling us to take courage and take heart in what He has already done. Christ isn't telling us to lie or live in denial, but rather to keep our heads up! Remain optimistic through everything and keep faith in God's Word. Nothing happens without God (at least) allowing it. So if God can bring you to it, He can also bring you through it! What doesn't kill you makes you stronger through the experience. Put that smile on your face today and be of good cheer. Live with joy and everyday will be filled with happiness.

Day 18

Oh Lord, Deliver Me!

> Psalms 40:13 Be pleased, O Lord, to deliver
> me: O Lord, make haste to help me.

Have you ever prayed a prayer like this? Lord, please deliver me! Perhaps you've been in a situation that was outside of your control or in a predicament that was pressing you heavily and all you could do was cry out to God. If you haven't prayed this prayer yet, then obviously you haven't needed divine help yet. But most of us have been in some things that needed divine intervention. Even salvation required divine intervention. As the song says: "I came to Jesus just as I was I was weary, wounded and sad; but I found in Him a resting place and He has made me glad." Most people come to Christ battered, broken, and beaten by the roughness of living in sin, but thanks be unto God for looking beyond all of our faults and seeing what we needed. For the record, deliverance does not always involve something major or cataclysmic. While most of the time it does; there are other times when deliverance can be simply a clear answer to a cloudy circumstance. When our minds are clouded with issues that are unresolved, matters that seem to have no end, or situations that don't have easy solutions; it's very easy to get bogged down. The weights of responsibility, the burdens of progress, and even the challenges of success (or failure) can push us into a deep corner of isolation and we thus need to be delivered. I remember back in 1989 when the Lord was dealing with me about deliverance. He would often come to me in my dreams. One particular night I was in a long hallway/tunnel that was very dark. There was a light at the end of the tunnel and I was moving towards it. As I was moving closer to the light; I noticed that there were cell bars on both sides of me. At first I felt compelled to hurry towards the light; but I decided to look closer and I noticed that there were sheep behind the bars. There were many cells and many sheep that were locked in those cages. It was dark, but wherever I looked a light would shine at that place. I could tell that some of the sheep had been there a very long time; their wool was no longer white but grayish. Other sheep looked like they were suffering from malnutrition because they were very skinny and feeble. I saw little lambs in cages with some of the other sheep. There was nothing but cellblock cages full of various sheep all the way down this hallway. I had absolutely had no idea what to do; but I looked behind me in the hallway and every cell that I had walked passed was now open and the sheep were behind me on the way to light. Needless to say, I didn't know what any of it meant at the time of the dream; but later I came to know it was the delivering power of God! You may be a sheep behind bars; but take courage because the Lord will deliver you too!

Day 19

God's Grace

> Genesis 6:8 But Noah found grace
> in the eyes of the Lord.

The word Grace appears over 170 times in the Bible. Yet it's interesting to discover that the very first place that the word "Grace" appears in the book of Genesis. Most people have limited their understanding of God's grace to New Testament principles alone. We focus on being saved by Grace all the time. Many of the Epistle letters refer to grace and peace in their opening salutations and through the letters as essential to Christian living. However, God's grace was present from the very beginning. Yes, Grace is in the Old Testament too. Even though the people of God were living under the Law, grace was present to help them. The passage shows us that Noah found something in God's eyes that nobody else in the world did. He found grace. At the time of this discovery, all of humanity was wickedly sinful and evil. The Bible says that all flesh had corrupted its way upon the earth. Sin is always progressive. It never stops at the first stage but continues until it has consumed everything up. We have to admire Noah. Can you imagine the amount of peer pressure and challenges that he faced by being the only righteous man living? Many people use the actions of others to justify their continuation in sin. I'm sure you've been in conversations where things are said like:

"nobody is righteous" – "everybody is doing something wrong" – "if others are doing it, I can do it too." Well, Noah wasn't looking at what everybody else was doing but rather he maintained integrity in the face of unrighteousness. God's grace found Noah because Noah was already living by Grace. God always helps those who help themselves. Grace is available for you right now. No matter what you've done, no matter how difficult your has become; just remember to keep accessing God's Grace. His grace does more than just forgive us; His grace sustains us. His eyes are in every place beholding the good and the evil. He is looking for someone that He can show His grace and glory too. Why not let it be shown to you? Do what is right, live in integrity, walk by faith, and find grace in the sight of God. You'll never be more blessed than when you know you're in good standings with God. Some people seek money, fame, fortune, and all kinds of natural trappings of success; but if you live with grace; you'll always have more than enough.

Day 20

He's Enlarging Me Through Distress

> Psalms 4:1 Hear me when I call, O God of my righteousness: thou hast enlarged me when I was in distress; have mercy upon me, and hear my prayer.

When something is enlarged, it is made bigger through expansion. In order for this process to take place, the object must first have the capacity to expand. Without the capacity to expand, the object would probably break under the stress and tension of the process. God wants to enlarge us in all kinds of ways. It is the will of God for His people to continue to expand spiritually, emotionally, and naturally. However, in the expansion, we must be flexible and willing to adjust. To put it another way, we need capacity. A cartoon of eggs that's designed for a dozen can only comfortably hold twelve. A five-gallon bucket has a capacity of five gallons alone. Anything over the capacity of a thing is excess and overflow because it would lack the ability to maintain it. In today's passage, the Psalmist learned through the process of affliction that God had made him a stronger person. He used the "past tense" of the word enlarge because it was the things that he had already been through that made him who he was. Most of the time when we're in the midst of distressful circumstances we are unaware that we're being made larger. Somehow God uses the worst to make things better for us. It doesn't feel good and it certainly isn't ideal, but God will expand us. Essentially the Lord is enlarging on our capacity. He is making us able to handle more than we used to. At the heart of the matter is our ability to comfortably manage the things that are coming. In other words God will deconstruct you now to reconstruct you later. Through the enlargement process, expansion happens. It's wonderful to think of challenges in this light because the focus is moved from what I'm dealing with to what is on the way. Yes, we are all being prepared for something greater. The beating, pressing, breaking and shaking is all for the making of your new capacity. If we would look back over our lives and be honest, we grew more when things were bad than when they were good. It was when we ran out of options or came to "dead ends" that we finally realized it was up to God. When all of our mechanical measures fell short (the things we could do with our hands) and our mental measures (the things we thought would work) ran out, we reached a point of dependence upon Him. We must learn to praise Him in our distress and prepare to be enlarged when we come out of it.

Day 21

He Heard and Answered

> Luke 1:13 But the angel said unto him,
> Fear not, Zacharias: for thy prayer is heard;
> and thy wife Elisabeth shall bear thee a
> son, and thou shalt call his name John.

One day I was in a very intriguing conversation with a fellow theologian regarding the importance of prayer. Somehow he was convinced that prayer never changes anything, but it only prepares us for what God has already destined to do. Of course, the premise of his argument is based on a flawed reasoning of deduction. The argument concludes that since God has already preordained everything, there is nothing that we can do to prevent, enhance, or even improve upon what is already designed to be. Therefore, since we can do nothing to change what will be, to pray is only to condition one's self to receive what will happen anyway. Indeed to a casual person, he probably would have been able to convince them to stop praying. After he finished, I brought his attention to Hezekiah and Isaiah and how Hezekiah prayed and God gave him more years to live. I also directed his attention to the scriptures that confirm the effectual, fervent, prayers of a righteous man avails much. Not to mention that one of the most famous scriptures in the Bible is in II Chronicle – "if my people which are called by my name would humble themselves and pray… I will hear from heaven and heal their land." Finally, after he had no argument with the first points, I brought his attention to when Peter was in jail and the church prayed until he was miraculously delivered. Prayer changes things even if people don't believe it. The passage tells us unequivocally that God heard Zacharias prayers and answered them. Obviously, he and Elisabeth both had prayed for a son for a very long time. I find it fascinating that God "heard" their prayers a long time ago; but when the angel was delivering the news of the answer to Zacharias; he used the word "heard" again. The implications are startling – the answer was given the first time he heard him; but the manifestation didn't come until many years later. When did God hear him? A long time ago. When did God answer him? A long time ago. When did God manifest the answer to Zacharias? When it was the right time.

Day 22

Be Salt, not Salty!

> Matthew 5:13 Ye are the salt of the earth: but if the salt have lost his savour, wherewith shall it be salted? it is thenceforth good for nothing, but to be cast out, and to be trodden under foot of men.

Salt is one of the most important and essential minerals for the sustenance of biological life. It seasons and preserves food, while offering an alteration to the taste of the actual food source itself. It produces a taste that is not bitter, sour, or sweet, but more in the line of pungent. Historically, Roman soldiers were often paid with salt. In those days, salt was just as valuable as money because it was a huge resource. Whoever controlled a particular region would quickly control the flow of salt. As a commodity, it could be traded for weapons, clothes, and even bartered for land exchanges. Roman soldiers would send salt back home to their families for the preservation of food in the event of war. With a way to preserve food, it would last 4 to 5 times longer than normal. There are over two hundred million tons of salt produced every year; yet only 6% is actually consumed by humans. Too much salt can raise blood pressure and increase the risk of heart attacks and strokes. So any one with hypertension should reduce their salt intake accordingly. In this morning's passage, Jesus tells us that we are the salt of the earth. Just as salt changes the "taste" of food when it is added to it and slows the deterioration process for preservation, we should change the world in the same manner. But too often believers are too salty to make a difference. Anyone knows that if you add too much salt to your food it becomes inedible or you can over salt the meat that you're intended to preserve and it will ruin the taste in the long run. So how much salt is the right amount? That answer differs from person to person and situation to situation; but the right amount will produce the right results. If your results are not as you desire, check the amount of salt you are adding. We can be salt without being salty. We can be attractive without being repellant by watching the amount of salt we're using everyday. Since we are the salt of the earth, let us pray that we can season others without ruining our testimony.

Day 23

Praying Instantly

Romans 12:12 Rejoicing in hope; patient in tribulation; continuing instant in prayer;

When think of things that are "instant" we associate them with words like immediate and quick. Things that are instant, don't take a much time to get ready as other similar things do. Much of the food that we eat can be bought, prepared, and served instantly. We have instant coffee, grits, oatmeal, and even instant pudding. The word instant is so much a part of our culture until we've become accustomed to everything happening fast. Fast food restaurants, self-checkout registers, and even ATMs are all designed to reduce the amount of time needed to make transactions. For the record, there is nothing wrong with wanting things instantly; but there are other things that simply take time. Time is a precious commodity that will always be linked with the amount that's used for certain things. We often say that people can waste time but this is only a figure of speech. It's not possible to waste time; but it's very possible to misuse time; because there's the same amount of time in every day, hour, minute and second. As it relates to the concept of things being "instant," the normal amount of time needed is reduced. When it used to take an hour to make biscuits from scratch; I can now buy them in a can. Instead of kneading dough and rolling a pin; all I have to do is preheat the oven; open the can, set the timer and be eating in less than 15 minutes. The passage teaches us that we should be continuing instant in prayer. To put it another way, we should be always ready to pray. Not only should we be ready but we should also continue in the state of readiness all the time. This means that whenever the opportunity to pray is presented; we shouldn't have to take 30 minutes to recondition our spirits to pray for somebody else. Prayer changes things, and if we're praying all day "instantly," many things should be changing in our lives as well. Continue instant in prayer today by praying about everything and worrying about nothing.

Day 24

Walking With the Wise

> Proverbs 13:20 He that walketh with
> wise men shall be wise: but a companion
> of fools shall be destroyed.

We can tell a great deal about a person by the people that they associate with. While association is not necessarily the only way to determine how a person is, it can however; give us some indicators to be aware of. An adage puts it this way: "birds of the same feather, flock together!" Of course this means that we tend to collect and gather in similar groups. We're more prone to consistently hang around people that we have familiarity with. This does not mean that we have the same behavior, beliefs, or character; but we simply have some things in common. The passage is teaching us that if we walk with wise people, we will also be wise. In other words, get connected with someone who is much wiser than you are and you'll learn to be wiser because of the association. If you're the giant among all of your friends you're probably not being intellectually challenged. If you're the smartest among all the people you're hanging around; then you're circle is too small. There's room to grow and there's room to know. So the real question is: "How do I walk with Wise people?" First of all, let's understand that wise people aren't advertising that they're wise. Anyone who is going around begging people to listen to them probably has nothing to say. Most people who are full of wisdom aren't aware of the power that they possess. Many wise people are going around every day leading normal lives with little fanfare and hoopla. So I encourage you to start by listening. Believe it or not, volumes of wisdom have been missed because nobody was listening. We must ask God to condition our ears to pay attention when it's time to hear. Secondly, I encourage you to remember. Go back in your mind and recall those conversations that helped guide you through tough times or gave you direction when you needed it most. Take note of what was said and how you applied it and then connect that to where you are right now. Finally, record all valuable information for your future use in a personal journal. It doesn't have to be a daily reflection or diary; but it can be a central location to record significant spiritual insights, dreams, messages, prayer request, and promises God has made you.

Day 25

Victory in Vigilance

> I Peter 1:8 Be sober, be vigilant; because your adversary the devil, as a roaring lion, walketh about, seeking whom he may devour:

Vigilance is defined as being keenly watchful to detect danger and being wary. When someone is vigilance, they are on guard against all kinds of dangers that are seen and in some cases unseen. They are also wide-awake and alert. Believers need to know that danger is always near. The enemy seeks to cause us great harm, loss, injury, and destruction. And because of the shrewdness of Satan, we cannot afford to be asleep during these challenging times. The Bible calls him our adversary because he's directly opposing our faith. The adversary isn't just trying to stop us from doing what we're doing; he's trying to stop us from even thinking about doing it. He simply wants us to quit. He doesn't care how nice our clothes are, nor how much money we have in our pockets. He simply wants us to give up. The passage tells us that he's seeking anyone that he can devour. He's a real enemy, with a real goal. The good news is that we can maintain the victory over the devil by being vigilant. If we can keep him out, we won't have to deal with what he's bringing. Far too often we allow Satan too much leverage. God has given us power to deal with all the wiles of our enemy and this power is embedded in the Holy Spirit's presence in our lives. We must learn to use the tools that God has given us with vigilance by extending our prayer life over areas that the enemy is active in. There is no fear in faith and no doubt in love. We should not be afraid to call the devil what he is – a liar. Be sober in your thinking and clear in your resolve when it comes down to vigilance. Stand your ground in full confidence that God is for you and no enemy can prevent His will from happening in your life.

Day 26

But Lord, I'm Trying

> Matthew 14:24 But the ship was now
> in the midst of the sea, tossed with
> waves: for the wind was contrary.

God is looking for faith out of our lives and if we have faith as the grain of a mustard seed we can move a mountain out of our way. But underneath the basic concept of faith is the reality of putting faith into practice. The idea is to make faith work or to answer the question - how do we make our faith work? In the background of today's passage, Jesus had just performed a miracle by feeding 5000 with 2 fish and 5 loaves of bread. After completing the miracle, He emphatically tells his disciples to get into the ship and go to the other side while he went up into a mountain to pray. But while Jesus is praying, a storm arose. Something happened between what he told them to do and them actually doing it and that "something" was a storm. The storm intercepted their completion of obedience because it hindered their progress. Life has all types of Storms. Storms can come in all kinds of forms such as marital, financial, parental, employment, and sickness. These storms can come at anytime; but they usually come at the times that we simply aren't ready for them. Sometimes storms come between the time of when He told us to do something and the completion of the task. The passage says: "The ship was now in the midst of the sea tossed with waves for the wind was contrary." Sometimes it looks like we're fighting a losing battle. In many cases the evidence shows that we're giving all we've got and getting nowhere! Many of us are laboring, working, and doing the best we can with what we have but nothing is getting better. St. Mark says that they were "toiling." Twelve men were trying to move one boat across the sea but it wasn't moving. Sometimes our best efforts just aren't enough. Have you ever become frustrated with trying? Maybe you've never been tired of trying; but when you keep trying something over and over again and it's not working; one day you may find yourself saying to God; "But Lord, I'm really trying." "I'm trying to do your will, I'm trying to be obedient to your Word; I'm trying to be remain faithful." I encourage you to keep trying. God knows your effort and He will meet you where you are.

Day 27

Multiplying and Increasing

> 2 Corinthians 9:10 Now he that ministereth seed to the sower both minister bread for your food, and multiply your seed sown, and increase the fruits of your righteousness;

There are four basic operations in Arithmetic: addition, subtraction, division, and multiplication. To multiply is to increase in number by multitudes. The dictionary defines multitudes as being in great numbers. We can conclude that multiplication is increasing numbers at an increasing rate. Unlike addition, which also increases numbers too; multiplication simplifies adding by doubling, tripling, and increasing the total number at an expediential rate. In other words, the increase is at an increasing rate that makes the increase much greater. Every born again believer who has walked with the Lord for some time ought to manifest what they posses. Since we possess the Holy Spirit inside of us; and everything that comes with Him; the manifestations should be evident in all of our lives. We should manifest externally what we possess internally. It is the will of God for us to increase in "seed-sowing" and fruitfulness. Fruit is the manifested product that symbolizes maturity in our lives. An increase in "seed-sowing" will eventually translate to more fruit being added on the tree. The fruit on the tree is the beginning of my harvest. Too often, we expect a great harvest but our trees are empty. However, before we get to harvest anything there must be something on the tree. So we need God to increase the fruit on the tree first and then we can begin to fill up the baskets and barn houses. The basket is temporary place of the increase and what's in the basket is sometimes immediately used. On the other hand, the barn house is the extended place of stay for our harvest. When things are placed in the barn house, they usually aren't for immediate use. What's in your barn house? Where are you storing your harvest? If your barn house is empty, it is probably because your baskets are empty too. If the baskets are empty, it's probably because the trees are also empty. If the trees are empty it's likely because you haven't sowed any good seeds. To those who have something in your basket, don't eat it up before you can put it in the barn. If you have something on the tree, fill up your baskets and take it to the barn. If you don't have anything on the tree, keep sowing good seeds.

Day 28

The 24 Hour God

Psalms 74:16 The day is thine, the night also is thine: thou hast prepared the light and the sun.

There are 24 hours in every day. Proportionally, 12 hours have relative degrees of sunlight; and the other 12 are usually shaded with darkness. Believe it or not, there was once a time when many small towns would completely shutdown when the sun went down. The grocery stores, gas stations, and all mom-&-pop stores would shut their doors and reopen on the next morning. I can recall very recently that even a popular retail store that has hundreds of thousands of customers each day used to close at 10pm. Now that retail store and most of its chain stores are open 24 hours. As commerce and the need for convenience began to increase the demand for stores to remain open also increased. Even Banks began to realize that convenience and accessibility made more customers happy. There are some banks that now have 7am to 7pm banking hours and are also opened on Saturdays. In an effort to gain more sales and to increase profits, many Fast Food eateries now have much later drive-through hours. It's all about convenience and accessibility. Yet, long before stores and industries sought to accommodate customers, God made Himself available 24 Hours of everyday. God never sleeps nor slumbers; He's made Himself available all the time. We serve a God that's always ready, willing, and able to minister to our needs. The passage says that the day is His and the night also. It really doesn't matter what time of day or night we need Him; all we have to do is call on His name. In the ancient days each city would have a person called a "watchman." The watchman was responsible for keeping watch over the city and to warn everyone if an invading army was coming on the horizon. The watchman was usually situated in a tower or on a high spot on the wall of the city. There were 8 watchmen who rotated everyday and they stayed on their post for 3 hours. In other words; watchman "A" would sit on the wall from 12am to 3am; followed by watchman "B" who sat there from 3am to 6am. God is the 24-hour watchman. He never needs to be relieved from duty. He's always watching over us and for this, we should be thankful.

Day 29

Humble Beginnings

> Luke 1:48 For he hath regarded the low
> estate of his handmaiden: for, behold, from
> henceforth all generations shall call me blessed.

It has been said consistently: "it doesn't matter how you start but it matters how you finish." There are countless successful people who had meager beginnings; but were able to overcome those obstacles to preserver and become the best at what they do. The NFL (National Football League), NBA (National Basketball Association), and MLB (Major League Baseball) are filled with athletes who started very poor but their talents propelled them to become famous and rich. Hollywood is also endowed with actors and models that managed to overcome the odds of obscurity and to climb the ladder of success. Many of our finest Medical Doctors had to eat peanut butter and crackers through medical school to become the "life-savers" of today. The world is filled with stories of people who have gone from rags to riches. The story of Mary doesn't end with her being rich; but it certainly starts with humble beginnings. Mary says her lifestyle was one that was of "low estate." Perhaps if we understood the significance of her remarks we would have a greater appreciation for her family's financial condition. To put it plainly, they were poor. In her day, there was not a middle class like we have today. There were only two classes: "the haves" and "the have-nots." The haves were those who were of high estate and the have-nots were those of low estate. To be of low estate meant that you worked hard for a living and would likely work hard your entire life. The have-nots were depended on the Lord for everything that they received. Most of them lived off the land and bartered and traded; to make ends meet. Every seven years the Lord would declare a Year of Jubilee to free up everyone that was in debt; but the financial condition of most people did not change dramatically. Mary's family had betrothed her to Joseph and collected a dowry; but none of that money went to Mary. She wasn't financially strong; but she had God's favor on her life. God used her humble beginnings as an instrument to make her name great to all generations. She will forever be known as the earthly mother of our Lord. You and I may not ever become rich and famous; but God regards our low estate. He's eyes are always upon those with whom the world discounts as the have-nots. Don't despise small beginnings.

Day 30

In His Hands

Psalms 31:15 My times are in thy hand:

Imagine the innumerable objects that you have had in your hands. I know it's impossible to remember everything but just walk through the corridors of your mind for a moment in review. At one point, when we were younger, we all had bottles, pacifiers, teething rings, and toys in our hands. Somewhere along the journey we we're given spoons, and eating utensils for the first time. After a while we were introduced to crayons, pencils, pens and paper all of which were in our hands. In the process of handling things we soon had more important things in our hands like knifes (to eat food with), books to read, and things made of glass. As time progressed and we grew older, somebody eventually gave us keys to the house and later keys to a car. It's simply not possible to even name all the important things that have gone through our hands in our short lives. We have no idea how much cash money was transferred through our hands and how many important documents too. Many of us were handed high school diplomas and college degrees as we walked across graduation stages. Some of us have been handed certifications, contracts, agreements, and documents that changed the course of our lives and placed us on a trajectory that has helped to define who we presently are. These things were handed to us; but what they represented meant more than the documents themselves. What's in our hands or has come through our hands can have a life-long effect, redirect our goals, and create long-term consequences and ramifications for our lives. How many hands have you shaken in your life? How many people have you touched with your hands? The sense of touch is more intensely realized in our hands over any other part of our body. If someone asks us to touch something, usually the first response is to use our hands. The passage is teaching us that God has our times in His hands. Of course this means that we're very important to God but also our times are just as important. If it's in His hands He dictates when it happens. He controls the "timing" of times in our lives and we control the use of the time He's given us. If we misuse the time He's given us; we won't be ready when the "timing" of our time comes. This day is in God's hands and it's our time.

Day 31

Taking Control of This Year

> Ecclesiastes 3:13 And also that every man
> should eat and drink, and enjoy the good
> of all his labour, it is the gift of God.

Perhaps one of the most overlooked keys to having a successful year is being responsible for our own actions. I can't count the number of people that I encounter each year who blame everybody under the sun for their current circumstances. They've become experts at transferring blame and deferring responsibility of their own actions. God is faithful and will do exactly what He says for us, in us and through us; but the insufficiency will always reside within us. We must take control over our actions, directions, and goals for this year. Don't expect to simply float to the top of the mountain with angelic wings; there's much that you will have to do. Either we will control our own destiny or somebody else will. If we don't rule our own mind, somebody else will. We must harness and rule our own passions, desires, and fears, or someone else will. The control center of our lives is our attitude. A positive attitude is only the beginning of what it will take to reach your destiny. It (the positive attitude) must be coupled with determination, persistence, and effort. We must gain control of our lives immediately, both directly and indirectly. Let's not allow anyone or anything to manipulate our time, energy, or resources this year. It's time to get some control because anything that is out of control is dangerous, out of order, and will ultimately destroy itself. There are four basic sources that have sought and will continue to seek to control you this year: Satan, other people, the systems of the world, and God. Obviously, Satan wants to control us to prevent us from moving towards our destiny. Satan doesn't need us to do his will, nor is he interested in making us his disciples; he simply wants to prevent us from getting where we need to be in God. He sends distractions in order to make us detract from the journey. People want to control us too. They generally have an agenda attached to their goals. Either they want us to do something for them that they can't do for themselves, or want they us to do what they can do but have chosen not to, or they want to use us by making us do things we nor they can do. The world basically wants to control us for financial, social, and temporal reasons. And God seeks to control us to do His will and to bring us into the place of His ultimate purpose for our lives. It's up to us to get control over the untamed areas of our lives and bring them into order this year. Don't wait until next week, next month, or next year – start now.

Day 32

Taking Control of Your Mouth

> Proverbs 15:2 The tongue of the wise
> useth knowledge aright: but the mouth
> of fools poureth out foolishness.

People judge us every day by the things that we say. Sometimes we're guilty of putting our foot in our mouth; at other times we can say things that are so profound until we wonder where did that revelation come from? I'm sure you can recall conversations that you've had with people along the journey of life that are fresh in your memory today. There are also people who can remind us of things we've said many years ago that we have long since forgotten. Words have power. The Bible confirms that the power of death and life is in the tongue. Each day we speak blessings and curses into the atmosphere. The Apostle James teaches that our tongue is a small member of the body, but it can make a very large impact. In fact our mouths can get us into more trouble than our money can get us out of. This is why we need to deliberately take control over our mouths. A wise man once said; a fool can remain unknown if he'd only be quiet. The passage tells us that a foolish person "pours" foolishness out of his mouth. When we speak, somebody is listening. Just because no one is replying doesn't mean that no one is paying attention. We are encouraged in scripture to let our words be seasoned, wholesome, and formed with the intentions of edification. The tongue of the wise uses words and knowledge appropriately. A word spoken at the right time, in the right spirit, with the right motive can really bless someone that's going through a hard time. With this understanding we need to take control of our mouths in 5 specific ways: 1) Control "What" we say – what we say can have consequences for good or bad. Just because it's in our mind doesn't mean it has to come out of our mouth. 2) Control "How" we say it – the cliché says, "it's not always what we say but it's how we say it." How we say things often determines whether or not it's received or rejected. 3) Control "When" we say it – this may be the most difficult challenge of all. Is this the right time to say what we're thinking or do we need to wait for a more convenient time? 4) Control "Why" we say it – even correction should be spoken in love. We should never intentionally speak to cause harm or wound another person's heart, mind, spirit, or character through defamation. 5) Control "Where" we say it – a private conversation should remain private. It's disrespectful to confront people in public with private matters. May the Lord give us more grace to become better stewards in controlling our mouth; our blessings and future is directly connected to it.

Day 33

Taking Control of Your Debt

> Proverbs 22:7 The rich ruleth over the poor,
> and the borrower is servant to the lender.

Besides the exception of spiritual growth, finances is one of the main areas that has limited God's people for years. We don't give like we want to, we can't bless others like we want to, and aren't progressing in life like we want to all because our finances aren't like they need to be. When your money is funny and your change is strange; all other areas of your life will be adversely affected. Many believers have dug some major financial holes that will require a serious strategy to get out. It's time to get your finances in order. Aren't you tired of living from paycheck to paycheck? Aren't you tired of having to borrow to make it to the next month? Aren't you tired of not being able to manage your money effectively and efficiently? If you are, let's get started today. It is easier to get into debt than it is to get out of it. Careless or unwise use of debt will eventually lead to financial difficulty, family problems, garnishment, repossession, or even bankruptcy. Here are a few signs that indicate you may be at Debt-Overload: 1) your debt load is greater than your assets, 2) you repeatedly use credit cards to get cash advances, 3) you consistently fall behind in utilities and or rent payments, 4) you do not even know who much debt you're actually in, 5) almost all of your current and future income is already committed to past debts. God has better things for us than living in debt all of our lives. Yes, He's a miracle worker and He can do the impossible; but we can't just sit around and expect God to write a check out to us and mail it from heaven. There are some practical things that we must do to start the road to recovery. The "borrower" is servant to the lender. In other words the one who owes is under the control of the one who lends. The one who lends sets the terms of which he is to receive his money back along with interest. Keep in mind that it's ungodly to borrow and not pay back. Only wicked people borrow and do not make good on giving the funds back to the lender. There is a BIG difference in "loaning" and "giving." So if you owe somebody (friends, family, associates, etc.) you need to pay these people back. Don't avoid people that you owe – go directly to them and talk through it until you have paid them back everything. Your credibility and ability to witness is limited and in some cases hindered because your word has failed if you don't pay people that you owe. Debt is not our friend. It drains our wealth and prosperity drastically. Of course there are some times when we must borrow and make long or short-term financial commitments; but let's make these decisions wisely and through much contemplation.

Day 34

Taking Control of Your Income

> Genesis 2:10 And a river went out of Eden
> to water the garden; and from thence it was
> parted, and became into four heads.

I've always had a fascination with how incredibly efficient and organized our God is. God made an ideal place, the Garden of Eden, for Adam, and later Eve to live in. It was an ideal place with ideal conditions and yet it had four rivers flowing into it to sustain it. Even in "ideal" conditions something was needed to sustain it. All of us need finances to sustain us no matter how "ideal" our conditions may be. The Bible said that Eden had one river, but that river was actually fed by four rivers that merged into it. Those four rivers were Pison, Gihon, Hiddekel, and Euphrates. As it relates to finances, rivers represent sources of life. They water the dry places all along the route and finally the entire garden. Your life is the garden that is watered by the rivers that are flowing into it. Financially speaking, Rivers represent revenue and currents represent currency. In order to keep a vibrant garden; we need rivers (revenue) and currents (currency) running into it constantly. In other words we need Income (something coming in). There are numerable factors that determine how much is actually coming in. Education, experience, skill-sets, career-choices, job location, and favor are only a few factors to consider when looking at your income. However, the more income a person has, the better possibility for healthy finances exists. Therefore we need to keep the rivers (revenue) running and the currents (currency) flowing into our gardens. Almost all of us, we have at least one river which is our full-time job. If that one river is watering your entire garden then you may be fine; but if that one river isn't watering your garden you need more current on that river or more rivers flowing in. Eden had four rivers flowing into it and each of their definitions gives us clues to what they did. Pison means "spreading, leaping, and overflowing." This river was overflowing its banks. Pison to us would be overtime income. Gihon means "bursting or breaking forth while deeply flowing." This river was very deep but it swelled at certain points. Gihon to us would be savings and investments. Hiddekel means "darting and rapidly flowing." This river moved very quickly. Hiddekel to us would be quick cash or assets that could be liquidated easily. Euphrates means the broad flowing stream. This river was very wide. Euphrates to us would be finances over a long term or over a wide range. Some of us may need to look at how we can get more rivers to flow into our gardens. Others may need to seriously consider rerouting the rivers to the dry places within the garden. Whatever your financial goals are; just keep the rivers running and currents flowing.

Day 35

Taking Control of Your Savings

> Ecclesiastes 11:1 Cast thy bread upon the waters:
> for thou shalt find it after many days. 2 Give
> a portion to seven, and also to eight; for thou
> knowest not what evil shall be upon the earth.

Saving and investing is a critical piece in getting control of our finances. By all indications, our generation saves the least of all the previous ones combined. There is a major need to start saving or at least to increase the amount that we save. Saving income we'll make our financial picture more complete. I know a lot of people will immediately say: "I can't save anything because my check is gone before I get it." Others may say: "how can I save money when I don't even make enough to satisfy all of my bills each month?" Both of these statements are more than likely true; but it's not always the amount that you save; but the way in which you save. Savings is financially defined as money that is set aside for future use. The most famous quote about savings is:"A penny saved is a penny earned." An earned penny is actually a penny that can be more valuable in the future than it is in the present. Accumulating pennies (savings) can provide a sense of security, a source of consumption, and a nest egg for retirement. Savings are usually placed with institutions that promise to preserve capital and offer an increase of interest on the funds. Savings may also earn fixed or variable rates of interest when placed in the appropriate place. However; some chose to accumulate large amounts of cash and keep it shoeboxes, safe deposit boxes, under mattresses and personal places. No matter how you do it; saving will become the base of a solid investment portfolio. You and I need two kinds of savings: 1) Short-term Savings also known as "emergency savings." This savings should be whatever you feel comfortable with. Many investment advisors recommend 3 to 6 months of your current monthly expenses. 2) Long-term Savings also known as "goal savings." This savings is strictly personal and subjective. Review your long-term plans and determine a future date that you would like those plans to reach fruition. Chart a course where the funds would meet the date. In other words if the "goal" is to save for a car and to pay cash for it in two years; by determining the amount you want to spend; divide that amount by 24 and that should be your monthly savings. How do we get started? Here are a few basic tips: use a piggy bank to put all spare change into it and place it in one centralized location, set aside bonuses and refunds, break bad spending habits, and avoid eating out, splurging, and emotional purchases. Of course changing spending patterns is never easy, but if you really want to have financial freedom, don't spend all your money – save some.

Day 36

Can You Be Trusted?

> 1 Corinthians 4:1 Let a man so account of us,
> as of the ministers of Christ, and stewards of
> the mysteries of God. 2 Moreover it is required
> in stewards, that a man be found faithful.

A key component to being blessed is the importance of being trustworthy. Can God trust you? Can people trust you? To be trustworthy is to be worthy of trust. Trustworthiness is a moral value that is considered to be a good virtue. A trustworthy person is someone that we can confine in as well as assign responsibility to and expect them to complete it without reservation. Most of us have very little trust in people. In fact our circle of trust will probably consist of less than 10 people at various stages of our lives. When we were children we trusted our playmates, when we were adolescents we trusted our peers, as we grew older we slowly began to be more selective in whom we put our confidence. Yet out of all the thousands of people that we've interacted with in our lifetime; only a select few will ever gain our trust. Essentially, a trustworthy person is someone that we can tell our worries and secrets to and know that they won't repeat them without our permission. In personal relationships, in order for trust to be earned; worth and integrity must also be proven over a certain unknown period of time. How do you know when you can trust someone? The answer is simple; by their consistent behavior over extended periods of time. Yet, thousands of people put "life-altering" trust in others every day with whom they have no personal relationship with. Doctors take the Hippocratic oath, police officers swear under oath to obey the laws of the land, and judges take their office to faithfully execute justice on behalf of all seeking relief – we trust these people. But this trust is a general trust that is formed over the "position" and not over the "person." Would the people closest to you say that you are trustworthy? The Bible says that a steward must be found faithful, which is to say he or she must be trustworthy! In other words we need credibility, honesty, and consistent behavior over time. Most people don't realize the value of credibility until they don't have any left. Our credibility and trust are synonymous. Gaining credibility and trustworthiness is like making deposits into the bank. Some of the basic rules of making Trust deposits are: 1) don't withdraw until you need it, 2) if you make withdrawals; make sure you put it back, 3) don't borrow against it if you can't pay it back. Let's build up our Trust account as we prepare for great blessings to come. Be truthful and trustworthy and God will begin to release more than you've been praying for in all kinds of ways.

Day 37

Ants in the Pants

> Proverbs 6:6 Go to the ant, thou sluggard;
> consider her ways, and be wise:

I have many memorable experiences with ants that include countless ant bites and stories to go along with them. Anyone who has ever seen ants in action have noted that these insects are among the busiest in the world. They are constantly in search of food, building ant mounds, and even finding their way into some of the most unusual places in the house. I remember the summer that I declared war on the ants in the lawn. After researching my strategy and spending a lengthy time reading the reviews of every ant killer known to mankind, I finally selected my weapon of choice. I made a short trip to the co-op along with a few other stops and soon I was back to begin the first assault. I followed the instructions as read and did everything exactly as I was supposed to do. I calmly waited for a few days before I began to take a visual survey of the damage that I thought I'd inflicted. Unfortunately, there weren't any dead ants. In fact, there were more ants than it was when I began the first assault. Unshaken and undeterred by this small setback; I moved to the second assault which consisted of additional pesticides. I was fully confident that assault two would produce the desired result of getting rid of the ants. Needless to say; after several days and a brief survey and assessment of damages; I'd made very little impact against the ant population. As my frustration began to mount I knew I'd have to go nuclear to get the results that I desired. There is one known ant killer that can truly wipe out the whole mound in one bound – gasoline. The only downside to the use of gasoline is that it also kills the grass around the mound and makes the yard look un-presentable. After careful thinking, I chose to go nuclear and went all over the lawn destroying ants. True to form in just a few days the entire lawn looked horrible. There were beautiful spots with pristine green and plush healthy grass and there were blank spots with burned up mounds. It was an awful site to see. Yet in my mind I had completely justified my actions because the results outweighed the means – no more ants (or so I thought). After all my efforts, the ant numbers were drastically reduced but they still managed to survive. It finally occurred to me one day that the reason I could destroy the whole mound and not kill every ant was because some of the ants weren't in the mound at the time I bombed it. I know it sounds crazy, but there would never a time in the summer when every ant would be in the mound because hundreds of them would be out of the mound looking for food at the time. The passage tells us to consider the ant and be wise. Ants are preparing all the time. They're busy, they're resourceful, and they're deliberate.

Day 38

Staying Motivated

> 1 Thessalonians 5:11 Wherefore
> comfort yourselves together, and edify
> one another, even as also ye do.

The challenge to maintain motivation is extremely difficult. When enthusiasm slows down and our expectations are not met, a sense of normalcy settles in. This usually happens as doing things differently and trying to enact change becomes harder and harder to do. Many people have not finished their college degrees because they lacked motivation. Others have not reached their goals because they simply lacked motivation. There are all kinds of factors that contribute to a person's motivational levels. God knows that we are fragile creatures and He promises not to put more on us than we're able to bear. However pressure, punctures, and problems can quickly zap our motivation and leave us right back where we were. Thus it is critically important that we obtain motivation from within and without. When motivation is from within it is called Inspiration. To be inspired is to be motivated from the inward workings of your heart, mind, or soul. These motivations are often personal pursuits that are fortified with clear thinking and hopes of brighter days. We can be inspired by an innumerable amount of things. In fact, some people find inspiration in very unusual places and then there are places that are just naturally inspirational. A museum, a scenic view, the wavy seas of the Atlantic or Pacific oceans, a painting, a poem, or even a good book can all serve as motivational tools. When you're at the point of giving up or surrendering your pursuits for this year; you'll need inspiration from within. There's also a second type of motivation that comes from without. The inspiration from without is Persuasion. Persuasion comes from the encouragement of our friends, family, and loved ones. We need others to keep telling us to keep going. The words of others can become fuel to an empty pursuit or energy to a dying dream. When we're at our lowest points of this life, the words of a friend can lift us above the despair. The key to obtaining success is to remain motivated. So here are a few tips in this matter: 1) Stay Positive – there's nothing as terrible as being negative (especially about yourself). There's a bright side to every dark cloud, look beyond the gray and see the light. 2) Stay Focused – never lose sight on the big picture. Most major accomplishments take time; and with every passing day, you're one day closer to the completion. 3) Stay Prayerful – listen to hear the voice of God. The Lord can speak in such a profound way until doubts, fears, and anxiety will all vanish. Prayer remains a vital component in remaining motivated. If you've already fallen off track get back up and start again. You can do it!

Day 39

First Things First

Matthew 6:33 But seek ye first the kingdom of God, and his righteousness; and all these things shall be added unto you.

Priorities have been defined as the thing that has to be done before the other things get done. The one thing that must precede all other things should be a priority no matter what the operation consists of. If anyone knew how to prioritize it was Jesus Christ. He walked with priorities at the forefront of His life and ministry. We are expected to pattern, follow, and order our lives after His example. This is why Jesus says; "seek ye first the kingdom of God." The word "first" means that it's number 1 on the list. Everyone wants to be first in almost everything they pursue. People remember who won, and quickly forget who lost. Trophies of consolation are given to 2nd and 3rd place but number 1 is given to the champion. For us to seek "first" also means we've prioritized our entire lives around this one thing. The letters in the word FIRST serve as acronyms for what God is telling us through this passage. F- Foremost: When something is foremost its first in either time or space. Fore is a slight abbreviation for the word "before." In contrast, the word "therefore" would be the thing that follows the "before." When we understand what is "before" we also gather what it's "there for." I- Important: whatever is important should be on the top of our priority list. Of course we must learn to rate the things that are actually important versus those which are perceived to be important. R- Responsibility: Too often we take on responsibilities that are actually not ours. Search your life and see how many unnecessary burdens you're carrying on the behalf of others. Once we determine what is our responsibility we can also rank those things into a systematic order. S- Significance: Anything that is significant is worth noting and paying attention to. The significant matters in life are usually those of which we take into careful consideration. The opposite of significant is "insignificant" which means it's valued less when compared to everything else. What really matters in your life? What's significant and what's not? Who is significant and who is not? T- Time: Of course, when we look carefully at our priorities; the things that we devote our time to automatically have priority. Someone once said; "you can tell just as much about a person when you find out where they spend their money as you can once you find out where they spend their time." Inevitably, time and money are inseparable. People get paid for their time and for how they use it. It is time to seek God first and to place your priorities in their proper place. If you put Him first, you'll be sure to reap the benefits of a wonderful outcome.

DAY 40

Are You Having Fun Yet?

Psalm 100:1 Make a joyful noise unto the Lord,
all ye lands. 2 Serve the Lord with gladness:
come before his presence with singing.

In 1979 in a comic strip, Zippy the Pinhead uttered the now famous phrase; "are we having fun yet?" The phrase was publically accepted as humorous and was soon popularized and declared by the general pop culture respectively. The core of its meaning is that previous high hopes are now being let down. It's a sarcastic remark intended to let others know that hopes of a fun time have not materialized yet. The word fun is an interesting word because it means to experience mirth. Fun is when there's a sense of enjoyment being realized by the person experiencing it. In essence, fun can only be experienced, although in many cases we mistakenly consider it as an act. For example if you and I are having fun, we both are experiencing enjoyment but usually there is an act that is causing the experience. Whether we're joking around (conversation), playing a board game, or riding horses; what we experience determines if we consider the act to be fun. If we experience fun when we're fishing on a lake; we'll likely tell someone that fishing is fun. What we really mean is the act of fishing was fun. If we don't experience fun when we're fishing; we'll likely tell others that fishing is not fun. In actuality, fishing is neither fun nor not fun; it's the experience that we have when we do it that determines if it's fun. We're encouraged to serve the Lord with gladness. Serving the Lord is a conscious act of doing. Too often we have Christians who are serving the Lord but they're not having fun. They aren't experiencing the gladness, joy, or excitement that they should. We are supposed to be "having" fun! We should be the most joyful people on the earth. We should be the most comforting and thankful persons on our jobs. We should be the most exciting people to be around no matter what we're doing. Make the best out of what you have to deal with in life. Regardless to what you're going through, don't let the devil steal your joy. Serve the Lord with gladness! Have some fun! 24 hours are going to pass by in this day, enjoy it. The Psalmist said – this is the day that the Lord has made, I will rejoice and be glad in it. Don't let life pass you by without having some fun along the way. In your own memory bank, the memories that are special to you usually have something to do with fun. Nobody wants to remember the depressed days of sorrow and the time you stayed in the bed balled up in a knot crying. It's too much fun out there that you haven't had yet – so let's start having some today!

Day 41

Working For It

Psalms 90:17 And let the beauty of the Lord our God be upon us: and establish thou the work of our hands upon us; yea, the work of our hands establish thou it.

Let's understand that anything worth having is also worth working for. Anything that is valuable has within itself a compensatory meaning. The value of work cannot be overstated nor understated. Since the creation of mankind, work has been a fundamental part of our identity. Work is the manner in which God allows us to experience the fulfillment of actualized production. Our God is a creator, and we are made in His image to make and work, with the hopes of seeing the fruit of our labor. In a contemporary sense, work is the means by which we accomplish our personal goals. Whether those goals are financial, economic, or accumulation of assets; work is the vehicle that transports us to that desired destination. Too many people have the mentality that they don't need to work for what they want. We live in a real world that has a specific set of standards that offer rewards to the owners and workers. It's an economic system that is based in the foundation of the exchange of "goods and services." The system is called Capitalism. Of course the system also requires consumers who exchange their resources to receive the goods and services. We are all consumers. In fact, we've been consumers all of our lives. But the owners and workers receive direct benefit through their labor. Every day, countless people go to a place of employment to work in order to get what they want and need in life. Often they are being compensated far less than what they deserve; but they continue to work because they want to operate within the Capitalistic system. In other words, sooner or later everybody will need "goods and services." Eventually we'll need food, water, shelter, clothes, and many other things to have and sustain a certain quality of life. Thus work is very important. Not only is work a part of our nature and necessary to function within the commerce market; it's also fulfilling. When you work for what you want, there is a contentment that comes as a result of that labor. There's really nothing that can replace the fulfillment of earning what you own. There are two important points of emphasis that need to be incorporated into this passage today: 1) Work Hard and 2) Work Smart. Working hard is not enough, because we know too many people that have worked hard all their lives and have nothing to show for it. So work smart too. Put something back for a rainy day. Don't consume everything you bring in. Don't live for today alone; but live for the future too. Work for it.

Day 42

I'm Working On It

Psalms 90:17 And let the beauty of the Lord our God be upon us: and establish thou the work of our hands upon us; yea, the work of our hands establish thou it.

There are so many wonderful things that we can experience in this life. The joy of getting married, having children, owning a car, or buying a new home; are only a few of those many experiences. We are creatures that are designed to seek fulfillment, whether healthily or unhealthily. We're also seekers of approval and greatly desire to be accepted by our peers. Our self-worth is often connected directly with "fitting in" and being a part of something bigger. The people that we associate with have the potential to influence us both positively or negatively. So let's watch the company that we keep. Doubters have a tendency to drain our faith, gossipers can kill our confidence in others, and "trouble-makers" may get us in trouble while they go free. It is certainly true that whomever we associate with will likely become the person that we negotiate with and take upon their behaviors. A strong-willed person can influence us to give up our hope in God and in the things that we're working on. Therefore you and I must remain focused on our goals regardless to naysayers and negative-minded people and keep working on it. Even when you're not seeing the results that you desire, don't stop working on it. Even if you have to restart all over again, don't stop working on it. It's far too easy to give up and quit when you get discouraged, but don't stop working on it. Many years ago, a college friend of mine bought a car that was severely in disrepair. He bought the car because it was very cheap. He planned on restoring the car little by little and as he could afford to buy the parts. He already had stable transportation so he didn't actually need the car to get around, so it was a pet project. From time to time I would run into him and ask: "are you finished with that car yet?" His reply would always be, "I'm working on it." This exchange went on for approximately ten years. One day I bumped into him at a church service and of course, I asked him was he finished with the car yet. I was surprised to hear him say that he'd finished the motor work and the car was running good, but he was still working on the body of the car. In other words, "he was still working on it." Life is just like my old college buddy's car. We have to work on it. There's always something we can do to improve it. Even if the motor (inside) is running well, we can still continue to work on the body (outside.) Our work is never done. Beware of people who believe that they've arrived; it's only a trick of the enemy. We all have much more work to do on our attitudes, hearts, minds, and goals so just keep working on it.

DAY 43

Working While It Is Day

> John 9:4 I must work the works of him that sent me, while it is day: the night cometh, when no man can work.

Life can be divided into all kinds of stages, components, and ranges. Someone once said that life is the cycle of the four seasons: spring represents our infancy and childhood; summer stands for our youth and young adult years, autumn is the time of mature adulthood and winter is the senior ages that finally lead to the close of our time. While this analogy has wonderful symmetry and similarities, everyone's life doesn't necessarily travel the path of the seasons. I think a more comparable analysis of life would be in comparing it to a day. Each day begins and ends in the cover of darkness. Since midnight is the ending of one day and beginning of another day, darkness always accompanies it. In today's passage, Jesus clearly states that "the night" is coming, and nobody will be able to work. If we were to compare our lives to a day, the nighttime would be the last days of our life, essentially from 6pm to midnight. Our infancy and childhood would be from midnight to 6am and our youth and young adult years would be from 6am to noon. The prime of our lives would be between noon and 6pm because it's the heightened awareness of who we are. We should be functioning within our true purpose somewhere between noon and 6pm. On average, 6pm is usually the time when darkness begins again. It seems to me that Jesus is saying when darkness comes we should have already finished our work. I think it's critically important that this principle is understood early in life. In other words, from midnight to 6am is mainly a playful time. Our infancy and childhood allows for mental and social development. There is very little work going on at this stage. Even our legal system doesn't hold children accountable for all of their actions during their childhood. But somewhere after 6am, more is expected of us. Certain behaviors and tendencies begin to be developed, and we gather a sense of the true person that we really are and what we want to do with our lives. From 6am to noon, we're also gaining our education, both formal and informal. Habits are formed, beliefs are firmed, and social structures are established. When the afternoon of life begins, we should be working. Ironically, there really is no specific age for these stages; but in general terms we should know when it's time to work. Jesus says during the daytime of your life you should be conductive, constructive, and productive. I encourage you to keep working towards the goals and aspirations that you've set for your life because the night is coming when you won't be able to do it.

Day 44

What's Your Plan?

> Proverbs 19:21 There are many devices in a man's heart; nevertheless the counsel of the LORD, that shall stand. (Proverbs 19:21 Many are the plans in a man's heart, but it is the LORD's purpose that prevails. NIV)

A plan is a fore thought. It's the process of thinking about and organizing a person's present decisions with intentions of a better future. It has well been stated – "those who plan to fail have already planned to fail." One of the greatest challenges that you and I have for our future is to adequately create, pursue, and complete our plans. If the truth is told, too many believers are coasting through life with no idea of how to reach their goals. They have many goals and dreams, but having dreams and achieving them are two separate things. Why is it so difficult to get the dreams in our minds into the reality of our lives? Part of the problem is the inability to connect the dots of organization and structure along with the "short-sightedness" of actually realizing what we're hoping for. In other words a plan is needed and time is needed to fulfill that plan. The key word is "creativity!" Creativity is utilizing the mind that God gave us by thinking outside of the box. By being creative we can begin the process of moving the thoughts of our minds into the reality of our hands. Yet in order for our creativity to flourish, we must have a plan to place our hope in. "We are saved by hope" which means we have placed our hope in the plan of salvation. We are also helped by hope when we make a sensible plan that brings us into a brighter and better future but we must give ourselves time for the plan to work. Give yourself time but also give your plan time too. Too often people get discouraged when their plans aren't working and in many cases, it's because they haven't given it enough time. There should be reasonable and ample time given to any plan along with patience and adjustments for changes. There will always be unforeseen things to occur that may throw us off course. Obstacles and roadblocks are actually common for anyone who has intentions on doing better or moving forward. Yes, anyone can complete their college education in 4 years; but be willing to give yourself a little more time. By expecting the unexpected, you're plans won't be ruined if you fail a class or are unable to complete your degree in 4 years. Of course this doesn't mean that you can't complete it in 4 years; but don't set yourself up for failure – give it time. When things happen that disrupt your plans, don't fret; make new ones. Nothing happens "exactly" the way we would like it to occur every time. What's your plan(s)?

Day 45

What Are Your Expectations?

> Psalms 62:5 My soul, wait thou only upon
> God; for my expectation is from him.

Expectations are things that we are looking forward too. We live in a Christian dynamic today that has created a misunderstanding of what really should be expected. Unfortunately, some Christian leaders have created a sense among believers that they should expect to be millionaires, wealthy, powerful, always well, and live a life free of troubles. At best, this teaching practice is grossly incomplete and has created unrealistic expectations that are disguised as faith. We now have churches across America that are filled with people who have unrealistic expectations of themselves, God, churches, spouses, children, jobs, and even their spiritual leaders. The higher the expectations, the greater the disappointments are when they are not met. Also, the more unrealistic expectations are the more deeper and dreadful the pain and despair will be. Unrealistic expectations are dangerously unhealthy and they have two extremes. On one side unrealistic expectation has dreamers. The person with dreams is usually the character that's going through life wishing that his or her life could be lived in another way. They normally have big ideas of getting rich quick, try to connect with people who are already successful, or look for shortcuts to get to the top. In their minds, they only need a break to get there. They sometimes even act like they're already "there" to their own demise. Anyone who seems to threaten, correct, or tries to bring those who think this way, back into the real world is viewed as a hindrance and is usually discarded or dismissed. Dreamers have big expectations and they are driven by the few stories of those who have gone from rags to riches but what they don't consider is the number of those who have gone from rags to wretched. While it's true that dreams are needed, there is also a need to work towards those dreams. Success needs education, planning, focus, skill-sets, patience, grace, and much more to produce. The other side of unrealistic expectations is despair. On one side there are big dreams on the other side is great despair. The great despair comes when those big dreams are not being realized. And they aren't being realized because they were totally unrealistic in the first place. Most emotional depression is linked to an unrealistic expectation that someone has thought long and hard about in his or her mind. The question for you and I is; what are our expectations? If you tell me what you're doing in a realistic sense, I can tell you what you should expect. Anyone who is wishing to be successful in anything should be laying the groundwork for that to be accomplished. Check your future expectations against what you are presently doing and face reality.

Day 46

Playing By The Rules

> Luke 17:14 And when he saw them, he
> said unto them, Go shew yourselves unto
> the priests. And it came to pass, that,
> as they went, they were cleansed.

Rules are the core components that allow us to have reliable standards of which to rely upon. They are the basic tenants of the law, morality, language, games, religion, and almost all governance. From the very beginning of creation, God knew that mankind would need rules. He quickly told Adam that he could eat of every tree of the garden with the exception of one. Rules are critically important for several reasons, but mainly because they establish limits as to what is acceptable and what is not. There was once a time when certain social morals were held in high regard; but now, many of the established and foundational truths that were the foundation of our civilization are being reputed. In other words, nobody likes rules! Rules seem to cramp our style and limit our freedom. Some people don't want rules to apply to them but are very strict when it comes to someone else. Truthfully, we all like the idea of being the exception to the rule. The idea of being the exception to the rule is where the "hook up" mentality begins. When you are riding the "hook up," you don't pay as much as others, don't do what others must do, and yet you still have the benefits as if you did. There is also the reality that some of us are just simply unruly. To be unruly suggests that we know the rules but refuse to obey them. Every day of our lives we have the opportunity to obey or break rules. Believe it or not, it's very easy to break a rule. Speed limits are rules. If we are driving one mile over the speed limit we are breaking the rules. For those who are salary employees and don't have to punch a timecard everyday; getting to work at 8:05 when you should have been there at 8:00 is breaking the rule. In today's passage, Jesus had healed ten lepers but He told them to "go show themselves to the priest." They needed to show themselves to the priest so that they could be pronounced clean and also be given a clean bill of health. By being clean these lepers could now reenter the public life of Jewish civilization and could participate in festivals, employment and every social activity afforded to the community. Even though they had received a miracle by Jesus Himself, there was still a need to follow the rules. I find this passage pivotal to us today because we expect the Lord to override the rules for us. No, you still have to play by the rules. Even if God delivers you, don't dismiss the rules of the game. Don't throw away the central components that give us foundation and structure. In simple terms, don't think that the rules apply to everybody else but you. Yes, the rules apply to you even if you're anointed, gifted, talented, holy, and blessed. Don't forget it.

Day 47

The Next Level

Psalms 18:33 He makes my feet like hinds' feet, and sets me upon my high places.

In many Christian circles, much is being said about "going to the next level." There are sermon series, books, and even workshops designed to help people to go to the next level. The idea of moving up is actually a part of the spirit of man. While a lot of attention is being stressed about the next level, I'm not sure that we always know what it looks like. If everyone were on different levels at this time; then for all of us to move to the next level would mean different things for each of us. So the real question is: "what does the next level look like for you?" Have you thought about what the next level is going to be like? Most of us believe that the next level will be less stressful and filled with more blessings but in reality the next level may be just as difficult as the level that you are currently on. As the old saying goes, "higher levels mean higher devils." There is never a time when we will be exempt from the attacks of the enemy. However, going to the next level requires hearing God in a new way. The issue is not that He has stopped speaking where we were; but where we are now requires a trained ear. Every time we move up in the Lord, the surroundings may not change but the sounding does. God also sends signs (sometimes) to let us know that things have changed.

Many people don't believe that we should look for signs. They take scriptures like; "signs are for unbelievers" and make it seem like all of the signs of God are for people who are not saved. Then there are those that take the scripture, "these signs will follow them that believe" to mean that a saint of God should not be looking for signs; but signs should be following him. They even use the scripture that Jesus said: "a wicked and adulterous generation seeks after a sign." There needs to be a balance in everything. Some people take things to the extreme no matter what it is, even the things of God but I also know that God still gives signs; and it's just not to the unbeliever, it's to His own people. Sometimes we just need a sign, especially when we go to the next level. Here are a few signs to look for that will let you know that you are now on another level: 1) Things you used to be able to do very easy, have now become more difficult to do. 2) People you were once close to are now seemingly farther away from you. 3) You have new opportunities along with new challenges that are related to one another. 4) You or your family is being spiritually attacked or you are being tempted in places that you once had the victory over. 5) It takes more effort for you to receive spiritual things (reading, praying, fasting, and meditation). Well, if any of these signs are happening to you, praise God because you are now on another level and there's more to come.

Day 48

Next Level Living

> Galatians 2:20 I am crucified with Christ: nevertheless I live; yet not I, but Christ liveth in me: and the life which I now live in the flesh I live by the faith of the Son of God, who loved me, and gave himself for me.

The word Christian literally is "to be Christ-like." In other words, if we are children of God we ought to act, walk, and live like it. To live right means that we are letting God live through us by becoming a vessel that carries His glory. Next level living requires that our will becomes God's will and our thoughts become His thoughts. Our ways and everything that we do is subject to whether or not God can be glorified in it. Next level living also requires that we should live by faith and operate with Jesus on our minds. Our prayer life is saturated with hope and our consecration is confirmed. Today's passage is the summation of everything that is required of anyone who is chasing after God. First of all Paul says: "I am crucified with Christ." Anything that is "with" something else, is accompanying it. We were "with" Christ as He was crucified even though we weren't even born yet. The crucifixion happened over 2000 years ago and only a few decades after Paul wrote the letter. Nobody seriously doubts that the crucifixion isn't obviously a past event in history. Yet Paul uses a present tense verb to describe what He was doing. He said: "I am" crucified with Christ, even though the event has already occurred. I interpret this scripture to mean this: Christ was crucified long ago in the past; but I am being crucified in the present with Christ. Next level living begins with us being crucified. Secondly, nevertheless we live. How can something that is being crucified still be living? It can still remain alive for quite a while on the cross. Historical evidence supports that a crucifixion was a very slow death that could take days for the person to die. In this case, we are only truly living while we remain alive on the cross. Thirdly, next level living requires a "yet not I." Yes we are literally being crucified alive; but it's not about us. It may be happening to you but it's not about you. It may involve things that pertain to you but it's still not about you. The phrase "yet not I" suggest that even though I'm suffering in this I'm simply a channel of which God can get the glory. It does hurt me but it's also helping me. Finally, next level living is "when Christ lives in me." I'm being crucified with Christ and He is living inside of me and because he is living within me, I can face tomorrow and all fear is gone. Really, the only reason I can handle being crucified is because He is living inside of me. If you're already on the next level, live by the next level understanding of this verse. We can never have a resurrection until we've first taken up our cross and followed Him.

Day 49

Pray Through It

> Luke 18:1 And he spake a parable
> unto them to this end, that men ought
> always to pray, and not to faint;

There are two powerful ingredients to being an effective believer: Prayer and Faith. They are fundamentally critical in our spiritual survival but also for our thriving. In order to pray we need to be motivated and there are literally thousands of things that can motivate us to seek God. Within the thousands of motivations there are two primary components that are headers of our motivation: Desperation and Inspiration. When we are praying from desperation; it is generally when things have gone wrong. As trouble comes and when trials are attacking our life, we seek for help. Desperate people do desperate things (including pray). People who don't have a serious prayer life seem to seek God when things are at desperate measures. Even our nation prays when bad things happen. After 911 happened, all of our political leaders asked everyone to pray and declared a full day of prayer prior to going into war. When the recent rash of school shootings started happening; no one was guarded against prayer in school. But these futile attempts at prayer are motivated strictly from the need of "relief" motivation. In other words, Lord I need help and I need it right now so move now. Desperation isn't the best way to get God to act on our behalf, but on occasion; God does respond to desperate prayers. Mature believers should outgrow a desperation prayer life and develop a more consistent means of communication with God. On the other hand, there's prayer that is motivated through inspiration. Inspirational prayer begins from a heart that is turned towards God with intentions of really getting closer to Him. You can tell how much a person desires to get closer to God by their prayer life. When something inside of us is compelling, desiring, and craving for us to pray – this is inspiration. To pray is to "call" upon the Lord. It's to make an appeal, a cry, or even a request. As our hearts are turned towards God our mouths will automatically follow the lead. Consequently, inspirational prayer will begin to build our spiritual character. We will become more focused, consecrated, and fine-tuned for service. We will also be more inclined to pray through our difficulties without giving up so quickly. It has been said that prayer changes things; and it does – but prayer also changes us. Praying through challenges actually gives us spiritual endurance. Pray about it. Don't give up because you're not seeing the results you'd like yet. Just keep on praying. Pray until your attitude changes about what you're praying about. Pray until the peace of God comes over your soul. Pray until something happens.

Day 50

Pray With It

> Luke 18:1 And he spake a parable
> unto them to this end, that men ought
> always to pray, and not to faint;

Indeed we are assured that our God does answer prayer. Yet, there are times when God seems to be silent. There are times when it appears as if God is not speaking or answering our prayers at all. Nobody likes to talk about the idea of questioning God; but secretly or openly; if we are honest; we have all wondered at times what was God doing? Even the best Christians can be overcome with the difficulty of their circumstances and may begin to wonder if God cares at all about them. Anyone who has spent any length of time around church people has heard the miraculous testimonies of those that God did things for. They testify of having a check in the mail, or a phone call that changed everything, and even a doctor's report being reversed; but what do you do when you pray and nothing changes? Out of every prayer we have prayed in our lifetimes; does anybody know the percentages that have been answered? We may be shocked to find out that a large portion of our prayers are simply unanswered or have been denied on the spot. Does God answer our prayers? Yes! But He doesn't always answer them in the way that we would like. None of us know what is best for our lives so we may be asking God for things that would actually do more damage to us than good. God is so merciful to us until He ignores many of our selfish requests or simply gives us what He knows we need versus what we want. When I began to look back over my prayer life I started thinking about all the things I'd asked God for during certain periods of my life. I was amazed and also thankful that He didn't give me everything I asked for back then. My life would be a total disaster if God had said, "yes" to everything I wanted. Even today, God still hasn't moved all the burdens, fixed all the problems, or calmed all the storms in my life that I've asked Him too. There are still many things that I am simply uncomfortable with and really wish that He would do something about. But over the years, I have learned to keep "praying" with it. When it isn't going away, or if it is progressively getting worse, I still have to keep on praying. I will admit, that there are many times when I simply don't want to pray about it anymore; but even if I don't know what's best for me, I can trust God to understand my heart. He knows us better than we know ourselves. He's patient enough to listen to our prayers and loving enough to say "no" or at least "not now." So if you have been praying about things that aren't changing and hoping that God would do what you want Him to do in your situation, don't be discouraged. God knows what's best for us.

Day 51

Keep Praying

> Luke 18:1 And he spake a parable
> unto them to this end, that men ought
> always to pray, and not to faint;

Consistency is defined as doing something in the same way for a continuous period of time. It is revealed in the continuation of the actions of the individual who is doing the act. In other words, what makes something consistent is the reliability that we come to expect from the object or subject of interest. Each day of our lives we encounter people that we rely on and come to expect certain performances from them consistently. We expect the mailman to deliver our mail. Some of us expect the bus driver to pick up our children at the bus stop. Employers expect their employees to come to work and do their job. Consistency also builds confidence in relationships. We simple come to expect certain actions from our spouses, children, and friends over time. When these actions aren't being performed consistently any more, our confidence begins to fade. God is a consistent God. Indeed God is good, but we haven't been as consistent as we should in areas of commitment, faithfulness, loyalty and prayer. I'm confident that if we address and correct our prayer life; the other areas that we're lacking in will begin to improve. Throughout the scriptures we see many significant people who prayed consistently. The prophets, kings, and priest all led lifestyles of sincere prayer. Many of the Psalms of David are prayers that are placed to music. Prayer is everywhere in the Bible but is it evident in your own life? There are four keys to look for as it relates to a powerful prayer life: 1) You want to pray – The primary reason most people don't pray is because they simply don't want to. Even those who know that they need to be praying, and have many things to pray about, just don't do it. 2) You love to pray – after you have developed a desire to pray, it becomes easier for you to do it and you grow to love it. Loving to pray doesn't mean you're seeking or wishing for something bad to happen to pray – no you're praying about everything (whether good or bad). 3) You believe in prayer – prayer isn't a last resort after you've done everything else. It's a priority in your life and it remains at the top of your daily activities. 4) Your prayers have power – a developed pray life is empowered by the Holy Spirit. Jesus said that the Pharisee's prayers were nothing but vain repetition of words. So the focus isn't on how eloquent we speak, but how sincere we are in our spirits. When we pray in the Spirit, power is present to heal, deliver, strengthen, encourage and to save. Don't stop praying, you may be one prayer away from the biggest miracle in your life.

Day 52

Loving and Living in the Light

> John 3:19 And this is the condemnation, that light is come into the world, and men loved darkness rather than light, because their deeds were evil.

In the human nature these is a resident fear of the darkness and of the night. Most scary movies are based on the concept that when the sun goes down; the monsters and bad guys come out. There is something fundamentally scary about not being able to see through darkness. The possibility that something can see you that you aren't able to see or something is trying to get you and you're unaware of what it is – is frightful. The absence of light creates a heightened awareness of some of our deepest fears. People with an extreme fear of the night suffer from the diagnosis of Noctiphobia. They are afraid to be alone in the darkness of night, sleep with lights on all over the house, and carry flashlights everywhere they go. Fear is a very powerful motivator. When someone is truly afraid, they throw caution to the wind and exercise the natural law of self-preservation. The darkness of night and the fear of night can also cause people to do things that they wouldn't normally do. Some have jumped over walls, outran people much quicker than them, fainted, and in selective cases even died. But the question is; "what is it that we really fear about darkness?" Is it the darkness itself, something that we think is in the darkness or is it the fear of our self. The Bible teaches that God has not given us the spirit of fear and that perfect love casts out fear. Ultimately, the true darkness of humanity is sin. Sin is the root of the fear within our minds. But there are others who are not afraid of the darkness but they love it. In the passage, Jesus is not referring to the darkness of the night; but rather he is talking about the darkness of sin. Because in the darkness of sin is the pleasure of sin; but it's also the opposite of what is true and right. We can't be living in sin and living in righteousness at the same time. Anyone who is living in sin (practicing as a normal part of life), is loving darkness rather than light. To put it another way, if we are "right" we're in the light but if we're wrong we're in the night. 1 John 1:6 says: "If we say that we have fellowship with him, and walk in darkness, we lie, and do not the truth." Darkness keeps us out of fellowship with God. Darkness is the place where there is no prayer, fasting, hoping, or believing. It's also the place where there is confusion, doubt, unbelief, and turmoil. We can never have the joy of the Lord if we live in darkness. Our lives will have no sense of direction and purpose without the light. Come to the light and live in it. If you and I would only love the light as He loves us; we would never fear the works of darkness in this world.

Day 53

The Light Has Come

> John 3:19 And this is the condemnation, that light is come into the world, and men loved darkness rather than light, because their deeds were evil.

All life, colors, and most optical vision rely on the presence of light. When God created the heaven and the earth, the Bible says that darkness was upon the face of the deep until God said "let there be light." The "light" that God made was brought into the creation long before the sun or the moon was given the duty of producing and reflecting it. Light serves as both radiant and luminous energy respectively while also making biological existence sustainable. The air that we breathe comes from light. Through a process of photosynthesis, carbon dioxide is converted into oxygen with vegetation and biological life receiving what they each need. The delicate balance of life is intricately dependent upon light. Thank God for light. We could not live in this world without light or its benefits. The passage is confirming that "light" has come into our world. Yet the light that John is referring to is not the physical or luminous light of the sun or the reflection of the moon. This light is also distinct from the artificial lights of electricity and fire as well. The light that has come into the world is Jesus Christ Himself. As the prophet Isaiah declared in his later chapters – "arise and shine for the light is come and the glory of the Lord will be revealed." Jesus is the light of the world. Actually, He is the only true light that comes from above and in Him is no darkness at all. The light of Christ shines into the hearts of men with the intentions of bringing them into the light. But because men love and prefer to stay in darkness they reject the light to live in sin. Are you living in the light? Do you prefer darkness rather than light? Are your deeds more reflective of wickedness or righteousness? The light has come and it's time to live in it. There are 3 benefits to living in the light: 1) Visualization - We can see where we should go. Through the light our vision is clear and our direction is known. We can walk in the light and not fear the dangers of the journey because we visually can see the way. 2) Actualization – We become as the light. Jesus expects us to let "our" lights shine too. Of course our light is an actualization of His light at work through us. The combination of His light and our lights together exponentially increase our ability to shine in darkness. 3) Continuation – Just as the sun continues to shine every day we too should continue to emit light. Some people tend to think that being a believer is a Sunday morning thing only; but this is a daily walk. Each day we must let our light shine brightly. Everyone will not accept nor embrace the light but we must continue to let it glow.

Day 54

Beginning Small

Job 8:7 Though thy beginning was small,
yet thy latter end should greatly increase.

Anything that is temporal has had a beginning. Scientists have discovered that matter, space, and time all had their beginning at the exact moment. However, the "big bang" theory, of which these scientists believe, is never credited to God. I've always wondered; how can time, space, and matter be responsible for the creation of the whole universe when they would have had to previously exist to do so. Who made matter, space, and time? In order for these things to collapse upon themselves and explode into a "big bang," they would have to be somewhere before a place for them to be was made. God is responsible for all creation. Whether He used a "big bang" approach or a slower process of creative construction; He is the only one that left a record and lays claim to creation. The Bible says "in the beginning God created the heavens and the earth." It does not say, in the beginning, people or committees organized their efforts. It does not say, in the beginning, money paid for this and that. No, it simple says – God. Sometimes in life all we have to begin with is God. We don't always have the luxury of starting off with money, support, education, or even knowledge of what to do. But as long as we have God in the beginning we can accomplish anything. It is better to start small. Things that start small seem to have a greater chance for survival. A small amount placed into a savings account consistently will grow into something larger. A small act of kindness can grow into a large return of the same manner. A small amount of leaven can make the entire loaf of bread rise. Small things are important in every aspect of living. Just the other day I noticed that one of the tires on our car was very low. I suspected that the temperature changes were what caused the loss of air pressure. So I immediately took the car to a gas station and refilled the tire back up with air. The next morning, the same tire was low again and I knew that it wasn't temperature changes in the weather but something was causing the slow leak of air. I quickly removed the tire and took it to the repair shop. It didn't take long to find out what the problem was. The repairman found a very small nail that had lodged into the treads of the tire. He removed the nail, patched the tire and I was on my way. Something very small had managed to alter my complete schedule for that day. If I had left it unattended eventually that small nail would have continued to leak until one morning all of the air would be gone out of the tire. Don't overlook the small things in your life. These things could be the very key to your future victory.

Day 55

I Shall Not Want

> Psalms 23:1 The Lord is my shepherd; I shall not want.

Because the Lord is our shepherd, we have everything we need. The scriptures declare emphatically that God supplies all of our need according to His riches in glory. There is nothing too hard for the Lord. As the Psalmist began to dissect his relationship with the shepherd, he began to notice that everything he needed was in the shepherd's care. God is the God of more than enough. He has promised to give us what we need, but also to give us many things that we also want. The differences between what we need and what we want has to do with necessity over convenience. In the King James Version Bibles, the word "want," can be misunderstood. It doesn't always mean what we desire, but rather in some cases it defines what we are lacking. When something is "wanting" it is lacking in necessity. The proper interpretation in this verse is: because the Lord is our shepherd we will not lack anything that we need! If we would be honest with ourselves we can see that nothing is lacking in our lives. God has been faithful to us in every way possible. He has given food, clothes, water, and shelter but above all, He gave us His only beloved Son. Too many times people confuse what they want with want they need. Because we live in a secular world that's filled with commercialism our eyes are constantly seeing more things that we want. Every day of our lives, we are bombarded with bigger, better, and more modern things. Yet these things are all going to perish away. It's not about who has the biggest car, the finest house, or the most money; but it's about who has the Lord as their shepherd. In trying times we all need to know that God is able. Life doesn't always hand us solutions to go with the problems that we face. When we face challenges and difficulties sometimes we just have to utilize what we have, until we get what we need. We have to use what we've got until we can get something else. In other words we have to be resourceful. God is a resourceful shepherd. He uses "ingenuity and creativity" to supply our needs. Sometimes God gives us just enough to get by so that we can make do with what we have. He gives us what we need by helping us to find practical usefulness with that which others would overlook or throw away. He opens our eyes to look at objects, ideas and people with a new perspective, looking beyond the present to the potential. When God is supplying needs, He gives strength to adapt, repair, reuse, or recycle the small things and incorporate them to our benefit. God is creative and finds alternatives even in the midst of difficulties. Keep your hands in God's hands and watch God supply your needs. Don't overlook what you've already been given – use it.

DAY 56

Green Pastures

Psalms 23:2 He maketh me to lie down in green pastures: he leadeth me beside the still waters.

Being a small-scale farmer and lover of outdoor activities; I've had the privilege of observing all types of landscapes and fields. When there are extended periods of time without rain, the ground becomes very hard and dry. It is difficult to till the ground to produce fruit when the conditions are so harsh. The absence of rain eventually causes fruitful landscapes to turn brown and die. You may have noticed that many lawns suffer significantly during the "dog" days of summer because without water, vegetation stops growing as it should. The passage goes to great lengths to inform us that the Shepherd has green pastures for us. Oh what a blessing it is to know that God doesn't have a plan to bring us into a barren, dusty, dry, and fruitless place. The Psalmist states: "he makes us to lie down in green pastures." First of all, we should take note that some of us need to simply lie down. Yes, we need to rest our bodies and refresh our minds. No one can remain healthy that works all the time without any relief or vacation. We all need time to reflect and rejuvenate our total person. When God "makes" us lie down; it means that we wouldn't do it on our own. Use practical sense when it comes to taking some time for "self-care" – we all need it. But what's even more significant is that the Lord designated a place that was green for us to lie down. In other words, don't like down in the mud. Don't lie down in the dirty places of life or the lifeless dry spots but rather come to the green pastures. The green pastures will have 3 significant identifiers within them: 1) Life – life abounds in green pastures. Whenever I've walked through green pastures I have always seen a large mixture of living things, from bugs, reptiles, and birds, to mammals. Green pastures are like a magnet to all kinds of life but they also attract the attention of regular people like you and me. 2) Color – the color green is symbolic of prosperity. It's also no coincidence that money is green too! When vegetation is green it generally means it's healthy and is receiving everything it needs to produce fruit. I see a bigger picture in the symbolism as well. We are to be healthy and productive in our lives when the Lord is our shepherd. 3) Growth – the pastures are growing and giving life as they grow. God needs believers to become life-givers as they grow in Him. When we understand that the Shepherd wants to bring us to green pastures; we too will want others to come along with us. Spiritual growth is the key to unlocking maturity in your life. If you can imagine the beautiful picture of lying down in green pastures in your mind, just think about how much more wonderful it is in a spiritual sense.

Day 57

He Leads Me

> Psalms 23:2 He maketh me to lie down in green pastures: he leadeth me beside the still waters.

Hardly anything is as important as being lead by the Lord. Everything that is critical to survival is predicated on the leadership of God. Under His leadership, blessings are distributed in wonderful ways; but being led by the Lord can also take us into the valleys, storms, and challenges of life too. When we are led to the difficult places, we can take comfort in knowing that those locations are not destinations but visitations. The Psalmist affirms that the Shepherd leads us beside the still waters. The image presents a picture of a sheep being led by the shepherd to the safest place to drink water. Still waters are not moving but rather tranquil and silent. It's refreshing to know that there are places in God's Will where we don't have to worry about the hurriedness or the quickness of a current. All of us need a quiet place to unwind. In my own life at times of great distress, I've found godly comfort beside still waters. There was an old song that stated – still waters run deep. In other words, we can find a wealth of knowledge and wisdom at still waters. Where are the still waters in your life? Who are the people that are filled with wisdom that you may be overlooking? There are four benefits to being led to the still waters: 1) Provision – not only is water a necessity for life; it's a natural liquid. Even though most of us buy bottled water, it's free. In fact every time it rains we are given a fresh supply of water. Without water, all biological and zoological life would cease to exist. We also need water to help us to remain healthy. It rehydrates our cells and organs accordingly. 2) Cleansing – nothing can cleanse like water. Each day we shower and bathe with it while also washing clothes and dishes too. Water is essential to maintaining normal cleanliness. 3) Refreshment – on a warm day, a cool breeze blowing off of water is totally refreshing. There's also refreshment in swimming or just putting our feet in the water. The reason most people plan their summer vacations around water is because of the therapeutic effect it has on the mind and body. Many physical therapists have now recognized the power of water and incorporated water aerobics into their client's exercise routines. 4) Attraction – a body of water can serve as a gathering place for all kinds of life. Fish live in it, birds fly to it, and all types of animals utilize it. When we gather at the water, we'll notice that the Shepherd has brought others to the same place too. The best place in the whole wide world is in the Will of God. Come to the water and find peace. Let Him led you there. I guarantee you won't regret it.

Day 58

He Restores Me

Psalms 23:3 He restoreth my soul: he leadeth me in the paths of righteousness for his name's sake.

To restore something is to bring it back into existence or into a former, original, and normal condition. Usually when buildings, statues, paintings, and other items are under restoration; there are also before and after pictures. The "before" pictures display the object in its deteriorating condition while the "after" pictures exhibit it in its restoration. Time has a way of wearing the newness off of everything even when it isn't in use. But when things are being used the newness is worn off at a greater rate. Our spiritual walk of faith goes through periods when we may need restoration. Most of us think of restoration along the lines of someone committing sin or doing an egregious act; but this is not always the case. We can be living righteously and abiding in the Will of God and still need some restoration. Because we live in a broken world, restoration is needed all the time. The Shepherd restores our souls. The Hebrew word for soul is "Nephesh." It has two main distinctions - the "inner self" and the "outer appearance." To put it another way, the soul is "what one is to one's self" or "what one appears to be to one's observers." Yet the basic meaning refers to the essence of life. As the Shepherd seeks to restore us, He is actually restoring our lives both internally and externally. It's important to grasp that life is more than what we do; but who we are, therefore we need to be refreshed and restored in our identity very frequently. Nobody can restore like God can. He is able to restore us in ways that other people will never know. It's interesting that David, who is the author of this Psalm, also wrote the 51st Psalm in which he stated – "restore unto me the joy of thy salvation." The prayer in both Psalms seems to be asking God to bring him back to his original condition. He wanted to be like he once used to be with God. I was once in a conversation with someone who wondered if it was possible for them to recapture the love that they once had for the Lord. They honestly felt that it was impossible for them to regain the passion and enthusiasm that they used to enjoy. Throughout the conversation it became apparent to me that they didn't know God does restore. The same God that saved us is able to reignite what we had with Him. Just like a fresh coat of paint can make a house look practically new, God can repaint His glory into our picture and restore our soul. When someone is restored they have the image of what they used to be, but also the excitement with it. The prefix "re" is to do again and in all of our lives we need God to do some things again. So let the Shepherd restore you again and get back to your original love for Him.

Day 59

The Paths of Righteousness

> Psalms 23:3 He restoreth my soul: he leadeth me in the paths of righteousness for his name's sake.

The beauty exhibited in the 23rd Psalms is almost epic in its imagery. Hardly any other passage in the Bible captures the full essence of God's relationship to His people like this Psalm. The Lord is the shepherd that's filled with compassion, mercy, and grace. Every detail of attention is paid to his sheep. Nothing is lacking or limited when it comes to substance and sustenance. Underneath the powerful provision of the Lord there is also a strong legacy of leadership. He leads the sheep in the paths of righteousness for His name's sake. We live in a culture that is determined to make what is wrong look right and what is right look wrong. Our society is quickly releasing the long held and well-established morals that help to build our nation. It's sad and tragic that righteousness is not looked at with a positive view but it's being held in contempt and disregard. It's refreshing to know that the Shepherd is still concerned about righteousness. He is so concerned until He is leading us down the "paths" of righteousness. Righteous is defined as being upright, moral, straight, and filled with justice, integrity, honesty and goodwill. Righteousness is also a character quality that reflects and individual's heart. And certainly righteousness has as for its root the word "Right." Essentially, righteousness is a reflection of divinity at work in the life of humanity. Our righteousness is only righteous when it is God's righteousness inside of us. Somehow many of us have confused righteousness with always being right. Fortunately, being right does not always mean we are righteous and being righteous does not mean that we are always right either. If we are always right, then we have no room for improvement. I'm very sure you know of some people who think that they are always right. Well, not only are they arrogant, but they are also blind. As the old saying states, "there's some good in the worst of us, and some bad in the best of us." In other words nobody is right all the time – not even religious credential holders such as pastors, preachers, evangelist, deacons, mothers, and leaders. Thankfully, the shepherd has plans to lead us all in the paths of righteousness. Even though the word "paths" is plural, it doesn't mean that there are many paths. There is really only one path of righteousness, but we have to travel from wherever we are to get to that path. That's how we can get many paths of righteousness. Each of us is on a journey to get to His path of righteousness but He is giving us credit for every step we take in that direction. Thank God for our Shepherd. He has justified us, consecrated us, and declared us righteous in Christ.

Day 60

Walking through the Valley

> Psalms 23:4 Yea, though I walk through
> the valley of the shadow of death, I will
> fear no evil: for thou art with me; thy
> rod and thy staff they comfort me.

When God leads us to places where we experience blessings of favor, excitement and overflow, we enjoy it. There is nothing quit refreshing as knowing that God can take us to wonderful places in Him. One of my favorite songs is "I Expect A Miracle Everyday," and I do. God is a miracle worker. Yet there are times when the same God, who is filled with goodness, leads us into the valleys of life. Valleys are not places that are particularly inviting. Most of the time valleys are positioned between two higher-level places such as mountains or hills. The mountains symbolize victory and achievement. Moses received the law of God on Mt. Sinai and spent a great deal of time communication with God in an elevated place. He also received instructions on the tabernacle construction will he was gone into the mountains for extended periods of time. Abraham prepared to offer up Isaac on top of a mountain. He had full assurance in God's faithfulness until he was willing to sacrifice his only son without question. Jesus gave the Beatitudes from a mountain and was later transfigured before three of His key disciples on another mountaintop. In a spiritual sense, mountains are at the apex of strength. On the contrary, the exact opposite meaning is conferred upon valleys. Valleys are not joyous. When most of us think of valleys in a spiritual sense we tend to lean towards hard times. The valleys are the low points and bottoms of everything we try to avoid. When we are having financial difficulty it's a valley. As relationships strain they become valleys. When high expectations are met with low realities these are valleys. No one can honestly live this life without going through some valleys. Even if God doesn't lead us to a valley, life will. Life is filled with valleys and they differ in length, width, and depth. For a college student, the valley may only be four years of intense mental development. For a single parent, the valley could be multiple years without any monetary or emotional support from the other parent of your child. For an elderly person, the valley could be the choice of whether to buy medicine or food. No matter what valley we may be dealing with the passage tells us that we're walking through it. If God can bring us "to" it, He can also bring us "through" it. Sometimes we just have to keep walking. Even though we're tired – keep walking. If we keep walking, eventually we'll come out of the valley. Too many people are stuck in the valley of complaining and murmuring instead of praising their way through. Every step gets easier if we praise Him while we walk.

Day 61

The Valley of the Shadow of Death

> Psalms 23:4 Yea, though I walk through the valley of the shadow of death, I will fear no evil: for thou art with me; thy rod and thy staff they comfort me.

Although everyone knows that death is inevitable, there's something that makes people think that it simply doesn't apply to them. In many ways death is still a mystery to humanity. The Bible teaches that death is a part of the curse that was pronounced on Adam in the Garden of Eden. Because of his sin he set the whole human race on a course that ends with every individual dying. I once had a conversation with someone who was very disturbed by me stating that everyone will ultimately die. For some reason, this lady had not processed the idea that she would soon meet the fate that is assigned to all mankind – death. Of course there is the miraculous exception of the "rapture," which is when the Lord Jesus returns to take believers away with Him. Yet even in the rapture, the scriptures say that "those who are alive and remain" will be changed in the moment of the twinkling of an eye. All indications suggest that the "change" will be very similar to a type of death because it will terminate our life, as we would have known it. As a Pastor, I have seen death in many lights. I've personally had several near death experiences, but I've also been with many people as they died. I've lost loved ones and many family members that were very dear to me over the years. My experiences with death have been numerous but also educational. The reality and certainty of death has taught me to live every day with purpose and intention. There is no guarantee of extended life, nor are there warranties on the people that we love. Each day should be cherished as a gift and filled with appreciation and gratitude. If you have family members that you've lost along life's journey, it is okay to grieve and miss them. In our human nature it is very natural to grieve when we lose loved ones. In fact it's unnatural to not experience loss when someone dies that is close to us. The body of Christ needs to recognize that even believers need time to mourn. Well-intended Christians can sometimes make others feel uncomfortable about handling the valley of the shadow of death. However, death and the subsequent grief that comes with it should be managed according to the Word if we are believers. Even though a void and sense of emptiness comes with death; there is a proper way to handle it. Walking through the valley of the shadow of death isn't easy, but God has assured us that He is with us in it. Praise the Lord that death is not the end of life; it's only the doorway into eternity. Always remember your loved ones that have transitioned and show love to those who remain.

Day 62

The Valley of the Shadow of Death

> Psalms 23:4 Yea, though I walk through the valley of the shadow of death, I will fear no evil: for thou art with me; thy rod and thy staff they comfort me.

Death and dying are not subjects that everyone loves to talk about but no matter how unpleasant they are, we must learn to share what we think about them while we live. For years I've been encouraging people to make sure that they've handled "final" business affairs before they leave. If you have assets, money, and/or valuables that are sentimental (such as family heirlooms) it is in the best interest of everyone that the owner decides who gets these things. When there are multiple heirs, things can get very messy really quick. I've been in attorney's offices with families who were in great disagreement over things that their mother had left behind. I've also been in courtrooms, family meetings, and in judge chambers as we sought to find a peaceful solution for siblings who were upset over things that neither of them had worked for. I simply don't believe that it's God's will for children to be fighting over things that their parents accumulated. The devil is busy and he doesn't care how sanctified we are or if we are educated or not; he wants to destroy the family. Unfortunately, death is one of the ways that he causes division. The Bible teaches that we should not grieve as those who have no hope; but we should grieve in the faith that the Lord will come again to receive us into Himself. The Psalmist says; "yeah, though I walk through the valley of the shadow of death, I will fear no evil!" In other words, I'm not afraid of death. Anyone who is afraid to die is living below his or her privilege. Life is short and filled with swift transitions. We should build our hopes on things eternal and hold to Christ's unchanging hands. When a loved one dies, let's celebrate their life by remembering the wonderful times we've shared with them. The devil will try to make you forget or make you feel sad instead of being filled with joy. It's ok to think about that person and laugh again. There's nothing wrong with recalling the funny things and the special moments you have shared with them and not feel guilty or depressed. The scriptures say that there is no fear in love and if no fear is there, then no regret is there either. Love again! Remember and embrace them but not in a melancholy way – with joy! Be thankful for the privilege of life and the time we have with one another. Today, make a special call to somebody you care about and tell them that you love them. Send a text, an email, or even go visit them and just let them know you are glad to have them in your life. The valley of the shadow of death can't be avoided, but it can be managed much better with the Lord's strength helping us.

Day 63

The Valley of the Shadow of Death

> Psalms 23:4 Yea, though I walk through the valley of the shadow of death, I will fear no evil: for thou art with me; thy rod and thy staff they comfort me.

The Bible teaches us that the last enemy that will be destroyed is death. This confirms that death was never intended for us. We were created, made, and formed in the image of God with the purpose of living forever. Sin brought death into our world and now everyone born will have to die. Throughout the history of mankind, death was a mystery. The Egyptians believed in an afterlife and built tombs that were filled with things for their Pharaohs to carry over. Many tombs in China also had sentimental belongings for their Emperors to use when they made it to the other life. Even though the Egyptians, Chinese, and many other cultures thought that they could take things with them; everything that they put in the tombs is still here but the people who died. Amazingly, the mystery of death was not fully understood until Jesus came and began to teach and reveal what actually happens. He spoke of a rich man and poor man each dying. The rich man opened up his eyes in hell, but the poor beggar died and was carried away by the angels into Abraham's Bosom. In the days of Job, he asked the famous question – "if a man die, shall he live again?" The uncertainty of death caused many factions of beliefs to abound. Some thought that when you died that was the end. They mistakenly believed that when somebody died they ceased to exist and it was if they never lived. Others believed that when someone died they would come back again as someone else in life. In other words they would be reincarnated again to live a different life but in the same world. Even the Pharisees and Sadducees had different beliefs that didn't coincide with what actually happens. When the Apostle Paul was stoned, he says that he went up to the 3rd heaven and saw things that he could not tell us. John the Revelator was in the Spirit on the Lord's Day and he saw the future of humanity. God revealed to John all of the things that will befall those who die outside of Christ and the joys that await those who die in the Lord. Yet even today the average person has no idea what happens to someone when they die. The believer should have no fear of death at all. Christ has paid for the penalty of sin for us through His sacrifice on the cross and we are free to go to heaven to be with Him. We will all walk through the valley of the shadow of death with loved ones and one day it will be our time to go. Be ready. Get your house in order and your business fixed so you won't have any trouble crossing the valley of the shadow of death.

Day 64

The Rod & Staff

> Psalms 23:4 Yea, though I walk through the valley of the shadow of death, I will fear no evil: for thou art with me; thy rod and thy staff they comfort me.

As we approach the scriptures to seek God's face, we must understand that each writer is trying very hard to put eternal truths into languages and practical terms that the hearer can understand. The symmetry and imagery in the 23rd Psalm is unmistakably geared to give us an understanding of how much care the Shepherd has for His sheep. There is no doubt that God loves us so much until He is ready, willing, and able to protect us. Every sheepherder knows that his ultimate job is to make sure that he doesn't lose any sheep to a predator. His skill set must be diverse in order to be able to confront all the possibilities that he may encounter. He has to use his eyes, ears, and special senses to protect the flock. There are two main tools that he had to keep with him at all times: the Rod and the Staff. The Staff was symbolic of his leadership. Whenever the staff moved; the sheep knew that they should follow the staff. At the tip of the staff was a hook that allowed the shepherd to hook the sheep to guide and steer it where he would. There were times when the sheep would fall into water and the staff was used to dip it out. Because of the wool the sheep has, waters could easily saturate its coat and cause it to drown. The hook at the tip was very important because it was used to snatch quickly or guide smoothly. Secondly, the shepherd had a Rod. Unlike the staff, the rod was not used to guide but to correct. Whenever sheep were being disruptive and disobedient; the rod was used to discipline them. Yes, I know we don't like to think about God disciplining us; but there are times when we all need to be put into our place. Rods do not have hooks like the staff. They resemble the staff because they are both made out of wood, but the rod is much more thick and heavier. Whenever a wolf is near, the rod is used to defend the sheep. I find it interesting that the same thing that disciplines the flock (internally) protects and defends them (externally) – the rod. The Psalmist says that "I will fear no evil" because God is with me. Yet he finds comfort in the rod and staff because they represent divine protection. The sheep, through trial and error, easily recognized the rod and staff. Too often we misunderstand God's discipline and mistakenly believe that God doesn't care. We need to recognize that God is watching over us like a shepherd is looking after his flock. His all-seeing eyes are in every place, aware of the wolves, and mindful of the direction that the sheep should go. We should praise and thank God that there's never a time when we aren't covered and never a moment when we're alone.

Day 65

The Presence of Mine Enemies

> Psalms 23:5 Thou preparest a table before me
> in the presence of mine enemies: thou anointest
> my head with oil; my cup runneth over.

Whether we acknowledge it or not every one of us has a real enemy. The devil is our main adversary and he seeks to steal, kill and destroy everything that we try to do for the Lord. Most believers are aware that something is against them, but they aren't always certain as to what it is. The devil uses evil spirits to help him in his efforts. Unfortunately, anyone who is not saved can easily be possessed with an evil spirit and be used to further Satan's works. The enemy also uses believers but it's mainly through manipulation rather than domination. In spite of all the efforts that true Christians engage in to keep the devil out, away, and bound; he manages to work his way into places that he should not be. He is in churches, pulpits, choir stands, church pews, mother's boards, deacon ministries, and even in children's church! He can show up on the job, the school, and also in your home. The primary way that he keeps getting into places that he shouldn't be is "through or with somebody." When the devil gets in somebody or influences somebody, they start behaving in manners that are ungodly. In most cases; if you are a true believer; those that the devil is influencing will become your enemy. Church people don't like to think of having "human" enemies but yes we do. There are people who don't like you and you may not even know why. You may also have spirits within people that are making them treat you different. Jealousy, envy, covetousness, and strife are human emotions but they are amplified under demonic influence. A person with the spirit of jealous can develop an attitude of hatred against someone and not even be aware that they're under the influence. Just as the sheep were in constant danger of being separated from the flock and devoured by predators; we too are under threat all the time. Enemies surround us. David was aware that the same person who invited him into the king's courts was also the same person trying to kill him. He had many enemies within and several enemies without (Philistines.) He was anointed but he still had enemies. Never think that because God uses you, the devil will back off and leave you alone – he won't. In fact the more God uses you, the more the enemy hates you and tries to stop you even more. Yet David says, God blessed him to be able to eat among his enemies and not be filled with fear, worry, or anxiety. The shepherd prepares a table for us in the "presence" of our enemies. We won't be able to avoid all of them. We certainly can't get away from everyone who isn't our friend, but we can learn to trust God in the presence of our enemies.

Day 66

The Prepared Table

> Psalms 23:5 Thou preparest a table before me
> in the presence of mine enemies: thou anointest
> my head with oil; my cup runneth over.

When we think about tables, sometimes we overlook the basic functionality of their existence. The table primarily functions to simply hold things up off of the floor. Of course, we can eat, cook, write, and use them for all types of things as needed. The first place in the Bible that mentions a table is in the book of Exodus. God commanded Moses to make a table that would be used to hold and serve the shewbread. The shewbread consisted of twelve loaves that were made from the finest flour. They were flat and thin, and were placed in two rows of six each within the holy place. The table of shewbread is a unique piece of furniture because it is one of only a few that was always in the presence of the Lord. The implications that the table represents are truly remarkable. The God of heaven desires for us to eat (fellowship) with Him. In other words, divinity is dining with humanity at a predetermined place called the table. Tables are not only essential to our lives in a spiritual sense; but they are all around us every day. Almost everyone has at least three tables within their homes. The dining area normally has one in the kitchen area, the informal den usually has one, and the formal den most certainly has a more expensive table. Incidentally, the church also has three tables. The table of the poor; where assistance is given to people who are hungry, thirsty, naked, and homeless. The table of the Pastor; where the Under-shepherd is given the resources he needs to do proper ministry. The table of the Lord; where we partake of the body of Christ through communion with one another. The passage speaks of a table that is uniquely positioned. The table in Psalms 23 is prepared by God and is in a place where we would least expect it. The Lord has made a place for us to fellowship with Him in the presence our enemies. Who would imagine that a table would be placed at the exact location where our enemies are? However, the purpose of the place where the table is located has more to do with our focus on Him as rather than our enemies. To put it another way, no enemy can stop God from fellowshipping, feeding, and sharing with us. Oh how marvelous this truth really is! It's great to know that God has a way to bless us in spite of obstacles and lift us no matter who is trying to pull or push us down. There is a table for us right now in whatever circumstance or situation we may be in. It may not be a formal dining area that has a centerpiece with fine china to eat off of; but it's still a table. Maybe it's a coffee table or an end table; but regardless to how big or small it may be, if God prepares it – it's enough.

Day 67

Thou Anointest My Head

> Psalms 23:5 Thou preparest a table before me in the presence of mine enemies: thou anointest my head with oil; my cup runneth over.

When we think of being anointed, most of the time we are referring to being chosen for the purpose of being used for the Lord. However, in Biblical days the practice of being anointed with oil was actually very common. The Hebrews anointed themselves as an act of hospitality (Luke 7:38; 46). The hospitality anointing also served as a means of refreshing and rejuvenating their physical bodies as they traveled from village to village. Even today the hospitality anointing is practiced among many Arabians. A second use of the anointing oil was for medicinal purposes. Oil was applied to sick people but not always for miraculous healing but for methodical treatments. When a person had an open wound; sometimes oil and wine were poured in separately or together. The wine was used as an antiseptic and the oil was used as an ointment. When Jesus told the parable about the Good Samaritan, one of his greatest acts done for the man who was wounded was to immediately address his injuries with oil and wine. A third application of oil was for when someone died. It was customary for many ancient cultures to anoint their dead with oil and spices. The spices would be blended with the oil and rubbed all over the body prior to the wrappings being applied. In the case of Jesus, there was no time to anoint Him before He was buried because the Sabbath was about to begin. It was unlawful to touch a dead body on the Sabbath, so the women came very early on the first day of the week to do what they didn't get a chance to do three days earlier. Thus when the scriptures mention the anointing oil; it certainly has a multitude of uses but the passage is referring to the seal of approval. Because the oil represented God's presence and approval, the high priest and the kings were called "the anointed." Anointing a king was the same thing as crowning him and when the Prophet Samuel anointed David; that oil was David's first crown. Another definition for the anointing refers to being "painted on" or "smeared with." Imagine a white canvass that has been painted on or smeared with red paint. We are the canvass and the paint is God's approval and presence. Without his approval we are nothing but an empty space with no color or picture but with his hands on us; we gain texture and meaning. Our lives need to be smeared with God's oil. As the passage says, he anoints our heads with oil. Thank God for choosing to place His presence on us. Let us walk like we've been smeared and painted with His divine presence on today.

Day 68

My Cup Runs Over

> Psalms 23:5 Thou preparest a table before me
> in the presence of mine enemies: thou anointest
> my head with oil; my cup runneth over.

Cups are small containers that are used for drinking beverages. Each day many people begin their days with some kind of cup. Some start with their very special coffee cup that helps to jumpstart their morning. Others begin with large cups of water or juice. No matter what our preferences are, cups play a major role in all over our daily lives. The Bible has a lot to say about cups. It speaks of the Cup of Salvation that is the thanksgiving cup of grace and mercy. The Cup of Consolation refers to the custom of how friends would send wine to console relatives in mourning. The Cup of Blessing, which is in contrast to the cup of devils, alludes to the sacramental cup of the Lord. The "portion of the cup" denotes one's condition of life and prosperity. When we think about cups; we cannot ignore the obvious purpose – to hold beverages for the purpose of drinking. The 23rd Psalm reveals how the shepherd takes care of His sheep. On the top of the list, a good shepherd must provide a place for the sheep to graze and a location for them to drink water. Water is just as essential to survival as food is. We need water when we're thirsty. It replenishes and rejuvenates the body, as we exert energy through work, play, and motion. God has enough to not only fill our cup but to make it overflow it. Usually when a cup is overflowing and running over it is considered a waste. Obviously God is not telling us to waste things, nor is He a God of wasted resources but we're looking at it through our limited minds. Yes, the cup is running over but the overflow is being spread out to other dry places in our lives. An overflowing cup is speaking of an abundance of supply. In other words, our demands can never exhaust His supply. Whatever we need, God has it – but also much more! He certainly can fill a cup with what He has to give. The earth is the Lord's and the fullness thereof! Can you imagine the God of all creation not being able to fill a cup? Of course He can fill it because He is the one who made it. When the Psalmist states: "my cup runs over," some theologians believe he's referring to the amount of blessings that he has already received and I completely disagree. I'm convinced that the cup is David's heart and the overflow is God's presence. God wants to fill and overflow our cups with His presence, not just with blessings. If we are filled with His presence, blessings, miracles, breakthroughs, and favor will also be inside the cup because of Him. Let's stop approaching God to get "things" from Him, but to get Him. If we get Him, all these things will be added unto us. If your cup is empty, don't start by asking for a blessing; ask for His presence.

DAY 69

For Goodness Sakes

> Psalms 23:6 Surely goodness and mercy shall
> follow me all the days of my life: and I will
> dwell in the house of the Lord for ever.

God is good! You've probably heard that statement many times if you're a church-attender. God is a good God and He's worthy to be praised! No doubt you can look into your own life and see just how good He has been to you. He woke you up this morning, and started you on your way. He gave you life, health, and strength. He blessed you with the activity of your limbs and gave you a clear mind. We serve a very good God. There are so many wonderful things that He has done until we could never tell them all. All of us have testimonies of His goodness. The Psalmist knew of how good God was to him and his relationship with the Shepherd was filled with goodness. As we begin to look at the last verse of this famous Psalm, it is no coincidence that we are reminded of God's goodness. We live in a bad world that's filled with evil and sin. Each day we encounter many spirits of wickedness that are out to steal our joy. The devil doesn't want us to enjoy the goodness of God and he actively seeks to keep us from experiencing His best. In spite of all the things the enemy does, God still shows us just how good He is. There are four components to God's goodness: 1) God is good all the time. Never think, because you're having a hard time, that God isn't still good. Remember, your situation could be far worse than it is. Circumstances, situations or predicaments don't determine whether or not God is good. He remains good all the time. 2) God is good when we are not. One of the best benefits that we enjoy in the Lord is His loving-kindness. He continues to look beyond all of our faults and sees what we need. We aren't always the best reflection of what a believer should look like; but He remains faithful still. On our worst days, He remains good. 3) God is good right now. We don't have to wait until tomorrow to see His goodness. Every moment of the day God is good. He's good right now in your life. Some people believe that there are only certain seasons when God is good; but the Bible doesn't limit God to a season. He's good whether it's winter, spring, summer, or fall. 4) God will always be good. There will never be a time when God isn't good to us. He's good in sickness or in health, for better or for worse, for richer or for poorer, until He calls us to enter eternity and beyond. Tell someone of His goodness today.

Day 70

Lord Have Mercy

> Psalms 23:6 Surely goodness and mercy shall follow me all the days of my life: and I will dwell in the house of the Lord for ever.

Mercy is compassion shown to an offender. Another word for "mercy" in the KJV translation is "lovingkindness." Jesus declared a blessing to those who were merciful – "blessed are the merciful: for they shall obtain mercy." A real offence is when someone does things to offend us whether through words or deeds. In this case it is appropriate (through a series of steps) to show mercy on the offender. A false offence is when someone is offended and nothing has been said or done to justify his or her feelings. The devil wants to get us offended. He works through manipulation to make relationships difficult to maintain. Slowly and surely he lures the unsuspected into the many traps of offence. We're living at a time when people are very easily offended. Some are offended over small, petty and childish things while others have a real legitimate reason for being offended. For the record, it needs to be understood that sometimes we offend people and we are not fully aware of what we've done. There are also times when people are just looking for something to get offended over. It happens every Sunday at churches everywhere. People come to church looking for something to get upset about, or come with itching ears. In spite of all the tricks of the enemy, if someone has offended us, we must (with the help of the Spirit and by the leading of God) learn to show mercy. Mercy has a working relationship with 3 major components of Christianity (Forgiveness, Love, and Grace). 1. Mercy and Forgiveness: Mercy and Forgiveness are different concepts but each depends on the other. God's forgiveness of our sins would not be possible without mercy. In the same way, mercy leads to some type of concession, which is usually forgiveness. 2. Mercy and Love: As forgiveness and mercy work in consort, so does mercy and love work in the same way. Love can function independent of an offence, but it is at its best when there is a need. In other words, love expresses itself definitively when mercy and forgiveness is needed. 3. Mercy and Grace: Mercy and grace are very similar with a few exceptions. Mercy primarily deals with some kind of pain, misery, offence, or distress but grace addresses the cause of those vices. Consider "mercy" as a treatment to an illness and "grace" as its cure. Thank God for mercy, grace, love, and forgiveness because without these we would be desperately hopeless.

Day 71

What's Following Me?

Psalms 23:6 Surely goodness and mercy shall follow me all the days of my life: and I will dwell in the house of the Lord for ever.

Perhaps there can be nothing as unnerving as being aware that someone is following you, yet thousands of people are being followed everyday for their protection. Our President, elected officials, and many other dignitaries live their lives under close observation continually. On the other hand, private investigators are paid nice money to follow people and collect evidence and then there is the unfortunate reality of "stalkers" who are violating people's privacy. Many people have fallen as victims to unknown assailants who followed them from work, home, school, or other places and committed heinous crimes against them. Unfortunately, countless lives have been lost, many are reported as missing and are never found, and some are permanently traumatized by the experience. It has well been said that behavior, when it is being observed, is modified. In other words, when people (even animals) are aware that someone is watching them; they act different. In a sense, it's very difficult to get the true natural interactions and instincts of someone when they know they're under observation. When it comes to the relationship with the Shepherd and the sheep; following isn't anything to fear. In fact the Shepherds watchful eye remains faithful towards the flock everywhere they go. God is not only leading us, but God is also following us too. I once heard a preacher condemn the song; "Wherever I go, let your Spirit follow me." His position was that we should not be asking God to follow us, but rather to lead us everywhere we go. While the minister meant well in His interpretation of the Scriptures, I believe he missed a vital and necessary key that can develop all of our understanding. Yes, we certainly need the Lord to lead us; but we also need Him to follow us too! Why not both? Well, the 23rd Psalm certainly appears to be endorsing the grand idea that God's Goodness and God's Mercy are behind us. We are being stalked, monitored, observed, and I dare say – followed. Who wouldn't want God's Goodness and Mercy following them? These two divine attributes are witnesses to a blessed life. Others should be able to follow in the same path behind us and receive the same blessing on their lives too. Jesus put it this way: "these signs shall follow them that believe." Not only should we have Goodness and Mercy following us, but also miracles, wonders, signs, and blessings. Look behind you and see what's following you. What kind of spiritual impact are you making on others? Has anyone recently told you that you've been a blessing to him or her? If not, something else has been following you and it's obviously not Goodness and Mercy.

Day 72

The Days of our Lives

Psalms 23:6 Surely goodness and mercy shall
follow me all the days of my life: and I will
dwell in the house of the Lord for ever.

Since November 8, 1965, the soap opera titled "Days of our Lives" has been one of the longest-running scripted television programs in the world. It has aired over 12,000 episodes which have encompassed 50 plus straight seasons and counting. Ted and Betty Corday originally created the soap opera; but the show was later edited for public viewing by Irna Phillips. There are 2 core families of which the show centers around: the Bradys and the Hortons. When the show premiered in 1965, it primarily revolved around the tragedies and triumphs of the Horton family. But most people draw nostalgic connection to the show by the words that are uttered at each airing: "Like sands through the hourglass, so are the days of our lives." These words are being said as sand (in an hourglass) is slowly trickling to the bottom of the glass against the backdrop of a partly cloudy sky. The imagery generates a thought-provoking truth. The sands are running. Time is moving. Don't be foolish and ignore the obvious signs. Don't wait for the sun to shine to do something. You may have to make progress in life while the winds of change are blowing against your direction. No doubt the hourglass picture can represent our lives in totality but in reality; we don't know how much sand is in our glass. Most of us are aware as to how much sand has already passed through, but no one knows the specificity of the amount remaining. I believe this is why the Psalmist says in the 90th Psalms, "teach us to number our days that we may apply our hearts unto wisdom." The days of our lives will be filled with tragedies and triumphs; but keep going on. There will even be times when the stress of the moment may cause severe emotional distress; but keep going. These are the days of your life – right now. You can spend them wishing, regretting, and trying to forget; or you can rise up and live. Things won't simply change because you don't like the way they are; you must put a plan with your passion. Today's passage says: goodness and mercy will follow us all the days of our lives. We can't control the sand, nor can we control the hourglass; but we can do something about the days of our lives. Start with each second, and appreciate every one of them. It only takes 60 seconds to make one minute. Don't take any minute for granted. In only 60 minutes you'll have a full hour. Do something significant in each hour your awake. Set realistic goals that are very achievable like remembering to whisper a prayer at ten minutes till the next hour begins. In just 24 hours you will have a complete day that meant something to you and someone else. What will you do with 'this" day of your life?

Day 73

Take me to Church

> Psalms 23:6 Surely goodness and mercy shall follow me all the days of my life: and I will dwell in the house of the Lord for ever.

The house of the Lord should be as important to us as our very own houses. It is the place for spiritual development and fellowship. It's also the central location where we praise and worship God. The church is where we make offerings and tithe but also where we exercise our gifts, talents, and skills. Every believer needs a church home that has spiritual leadership. Within the church, relationships are built that are eternal. It's the gathering place for doctrine, disciple, and direction. There are two types of churches: one is the Universal Church and the other is the Tangible Church. The Universal Church is the spiritual body of baptized believers who have accepted Jesus Christ as their Lord and Savior. The Tangible Church is a physical building comprised of people who join together for various reasons. The Universal church is not divided but the tangible church is divided by denominations, agendas, traditions, confused concepts, egos and personalities. It is often within the Tangible Church that we have misunderstandings of what the church is all about. People can belong to a Tangible church and never know what we really have been called to do. Statistics suggest that about 95% of church attendants have misconceptions as to what the top five priorities of the church should be. Other statistics confirm that approximately 20% of congregants have a working-definition of the purpose of their church. Part of the reason why we have so much confusion is because of ignorance of the Word of God. However, the Church's mission is actually very simple. We are to be the Godly agents on earth that are representatives of what Christ would do if He were here in the flesh. We are also commissioned to preach the Word, the Gospel, and the Revelation of Christ to every creature and to make, train, and equip disciples for Christ. We are to edify the body of Christ until we all come together in the unity of the faith as one. Today's passage looks at the delight that we should have as Christians when it comes to going to church. "I was glad when they said unto me let us go into the house of the Lord!" I love church! I love coming and going to church! I love worshiping at church! I love seeing the people of God at church! I enjoy the Holy Spirit's presence at church! I love being at church. If you don't love church now, how will you enjoy heaven? Church is a rehearsal of what heaven will be like when we get there. There will be praise, worship, thanksgiving, joy, excitement, other saints, the Holy Spirit, Jesus, God, and many more delightful things. Get excited about church and start being faithful in attendance.

Day 74

Be Faithful

> Revelation 2:10 Fear none of those things which thou shalt suffer: behold, the devil shall cast some of you into prison, that ye may be tried; and ye shall have tribulation ten days: be thou faithful unto death, and I will give thee a crown of life.

Faithfulness is one of the most important elements the Christian faith. Without faith it is impossible to please God. Faith is the core of everything that pertains to God. The Bible teaches that whoever comes to God must believe that He is and that He will reward those that diligently seek Him. Hebrews 11:1 says "now faith is the substance of things hoped for, the evidence of things not seen." Since faith is the core of Christianity, it is also the cause and the completion of our hope. God is displeased if we do not have faith in His Word. If we have faith as a grain of mustard seed, we can speak to the mountains in our lives and command them to be removed. By faith, we can call those things that are not as though they are. It takes faith to be blessed. It takes faith to be healed. It takes faith to prosper and to go higher in the Lord. No matter how tough things may be in your life right now, we still have to believe what God is showing us. Whose report will you believe? Believe the promises of God. Believe the Word of God. In order to receive, we must believe!

Faith without works is dead! Quicken your faith today and believe what He says. We can't receive what we do not believe by faith and we cannot give what we have not received. We can't guide others where we have not been guided ourselves. Jesus put it this way; the blind cannot lead the blind. In other words, the lost can't lead the found. There are essentially three ways that we form our belief system: 1) We believe what we have heard & learned from other people – All of our lives people have been teaching, training, and showing us how to do things. Almost without question, we owe a great debt to people who have shared knowledge and wisdom with us through the years. Thank God for teachers who devote their lives to make careers of educating others. 2) We believe what we have learned through our own experiments – an experiment is a test or an attempt to try something to discover the truth about it. A large portion of what we believe is learned through discovery. 3) We believe what we believe through our own experience – all of our experiences have not come through trial and error but some experiences have been experienced by being thrust into the middle of something that was already in progress. Experience can be a great teacher, but it can also be very expensive, damaging, and can cause a great loss of time. No matter how we learn to believe; the important thing is to keep faith in God.

Day 75

Be Committed

>Revelation 2:10 Fear none of those things which thou shalt suffer: behold, the devil shall cast some of you into prison, that ye may be tried; and ye shall have tribulation ten days: be thou faithful unto death, and I will give thee a crown of life.

The idea of being "tried" is not something that many are volunteering to do. Being "tried" means that we are being tested, proven, and weighed in the balances. Every day of our lives we are being tested to some extent. We simply cannot go through this life without some type of situation challenging us. It is easy to get discouraged and begin to feel that you are the only one going through hard times. In reality, everybody is dealing with something. Sometimes what is big to one person is not as big to another but no matter how we feel about it; we must remain faithful. In today's passage, Jesus confirms to the church at Smyrna that many of them would have to suffer greatly for His sake. He said that some had the fate of prison time awaiting them. Prisons in those days were nothing like ours today. They didn't have three square meals, visitations, and plush accommodations. Prisoners were treated with great contempt and disdain. There was nothing to prevent prison guards from abusing them or even taking their lives. Christians would suffer more greatly than average prisoners because of their faith in Christ. Nevertheless, Jesus warns them that there were going to be some tough days ahead. Hardships awaited them, persecution was on the road ahead, and danger was going to be all around them. He directly told them "thou shall suffer." Wow! Imagine a message coming from Jesus that we were about to suffer greatly. Most of us would rebuke the devil and dismiss all notions that any kind of suffering was in God's plan for our lives. Yet, in reality nobody is exempt from going through. We will be tried, yes we will be persecuted, yes we will be torn, beaten, and afflicted; but be faithful! Stay committed! Stay in the fight! You can't give up now! Be loyal unto death! Be willing to go all the way with your faith. Others may never understand you, your family may abandon you, and your connections may all be discontinued; but remain faithful! Go in God's strength until the end. The most blessed part of the verse is when Jesus says; you will have tribulation for ten days. There is a limit to how long God will let you suffer. I don't know how long your ten days will be. Ten days may feel like an eternity; but there is a maximum capacity of suffering that God will allow. I'm so thankful for God's promise to never put more on us than we're able to bare, what about you?

Day 76

Be Prepared

> Amos 4:12 Therefore thus will I do unto thee, O Israel: and because I will do this unto thee, prepare to meet thy God, O Israel.

Heaven is a prepared place for a prepared people. There will be nobody who accidentally ends up in heaven with the Lord. Those that make it in will have made the choice to accept Jesus Christ as their personal Lord and Savior. Preparation is something that we do each and every day. We prepare to go to work, sometimes by getting started the night before. We iron our clothes, set out things will need to remember, and mentally plan our days out in our minds. Those of us with children know the value in preparation. During school months, it would be complete chaos for many of our households if there were little or no preparation for the following day. Homework review, becoming briefed on upcoming events, and simply following the progress of your child's education is a job that is unending during grade school years. Usually there is a direct relationship with the amount of time spent in preparation to the cumulative results achieved. In other words the more effort and energy that is put into something plays a large part in what we get out of it. The passage reveals the need to prepare to meet God. I couldn't imagine a scenario of which I would have an appointment to meet with someone influential and not be prepared. As a general rule of thumb; whenever you are meeting with someone of significance; don't waste his or her time. Most people with responsibility are busy with those responsibilities. When we are being viewed as an exception to their schedule please don't waste their time. We should have whatever we need to ask, say, or do already organized in a manner that is simple to understand. If you can't explain it in simple terms it's not time to share it with someone else. Secondly, know the facts. Never come with incomplete information or something that you haven't thought through yourself. When you are relying on what you've been told by others or hearsay; you may end up being embarrassed before it's over, so be diligent enough to do your own research. Yes, preparation requires diligence, but it also requires studiousness. God will not let anything slip up on any of His true children. He is preparing us for things that have not happened yet. In fact, this is the training ground for our next blessing. Our questions today will be our answers tomorrow. Our hardships today will be our miracles tomorrow. Our heartbreak today will be our hallelujah tomorrow. Be prepared so when things turn around, you'll be ready.

Day 77

Be Thankful

Psalms 136:1 O give thanks unto the Lord; for he is good: for his mercy endureth for ever.

Thanksgiving is a type of praise that should be without ceasing, spontaneous, and sincere. The act of giving thanks will show up in our emotions, actions, and attitudes. Anyone who is thankful will be grateful for what they have received. Yes, we should be expressive about what the Lord has done for us. There is absolutely nothing wrong with being forthright and forward about God's goodness to you. Never let anyone cause you to feel ashamed about praising God out loud or being emotionally expressive about His wondrous works on your behalf. The Bible teaches that the last days will be filled with a spirit of ungratefulness even among the saints of God. There are many reasons why we are not thankful anymore and don't appreciate what we have; but six reasons really standout above all others: 1) we do not tend to appreciate things when we actually don't need them. This is why the distinction between "needs" and "wants" needs to be clarified. We can buy all kinds of things that we want (at the time we bought them) but later these things are of little value to us. Why; because it's not something that we actually needed. 2) We do not usually appreciate things that other people have paid for. When it doesn't cost us; we haven't been financially affected by the purchase and it doesn't mean as much to us as it would to them. 3) We do not usually appreciate something that we have no use of. Have you ever been given a gift that you simply couldn't use? Sometimes people buy us things that they want us to have; but we not only can't use it; we normally don't ever use them. 4) We also don't appreciate things that we don't know how to use. Instead of tearing something up we simple don't use it. I remember when VCRs (Video Cassette Recorders) used to be so difficult to program. Most people never figured out how to set the clocks and so it just blinked 12:00 constantly. 5) We don't appreciate things that we have too much of. When our closets are running over with clothes or our shoes are too many to number; we don't appreciate them as someone who doesn't have but one pair. We throw away food that others would do anything to have. We flush more water through our toilets than some people have in an entire year to drink. 6) We usually don't appreciate things that have become "common" to us. When we are used to people, places, or things it's easy to start taking them for granted. I encourage you today to be thankful and be grateful. Appreciate what God has done and is doing; but also appreciate the people that He's placed there to be a blessing to you.

Day 78

Be Holy

> 1 Peter 1:16 Because it is written,
> Be ye holy; for I am holy.

Holiness is not supposed to be an option for the people of the Lord. When God first called Abraham out from among his family, He intended for him to be different from all other people. God also gave Moses commandments and laws with the intentions of providing a platform for what He expected of them. God wanted His people to be consecrated for His glory. He wanted them to be an example of righteousness among unrighteous people and to exhibit goodness in an evil world. Indeed the task would be great to do, but if they had obeyed, the Nation would have easily risen higher than any other nation on the earth. The challenge for them back then is the same challenge for us today. We should live holy because God expects us to and not because of rules or regulations. Unfortunately, most people have a terrible conception of holiness. It isn't being weird, unpredictable, and judgmental; neither is it all about how we dress, whether or not we have long or short hair, or what our denomination is. Holiness is a commitment to God's godly principles for living righteous. So we must change the way we think about God and what He expects. Even though we are under the New Covenant of grace and mercy we do not have a license to sin. We simply can't go out and do whatever we want to do under the name of Jesus Christ. The world is watching us. Almost all of us know of folks who are very good hypocrites. In fact, they sometimes will even get up and say how wrong they have been living, but God knows their heart. For some reason, I have never been a fan of people playing these games in church. In my opinion, the hypocrite is missing out on the best part of God by living a lifestyle contrary to His will. The Bible tells us to be holy because God is holy. Of course, our holiness is unlike God's in several ways. First of all, God's holiness is perfect holiness. He is the only one that is Holy, Holy, Holy. He is completely beyond sin, unrighteousness, and evil. God is the perfection of perfection and the essence of all that is good. Our holiness can never come close to His holiness. Secondly, our holiness is a shared holiness. God has given us His holiness in His Son Jesus Christ. We are heirs and joint heirs with Christ and are partakers in His divine nature through the Cross. We owe Him great praise for His wonderful salvation that is given to us. Thirdly, our holiness is progressive sanctification. In other words, we should be growing closer and becoming more like Jesus every day. We should be doing what is right, good, and godly continuously. In your own life, examine the areas where you aren't living holy and do something about it. Make some changes and come closer to the Cross.

Day 79

Be Glad

Psalms 118:24 This is the day which the Lord hath made; we will rejoice and be glad in it.

A lifetime is a long time to be miserable. Someone once wrote, unhappy people are usually unhappy because they have not mastered the ability to be happy within themselves. We all want to be happy in some way or another. We strive, seek, and desire to have happiness even though we aren't sure exactly how to obtain it. Happiness is both an emotion and a state of being. In other words, a person can be happy even though they aren't experiencing a sensation to stimulate that emotion. To be glad is to be happy about something that is occurring. Obviously, God does not want us to live in misery and defeat; and by contrast, we should be happy people. The Bible says that the joy of the Lord is our strength. We have a growing assurance that God wishes for us to be people who exhibit His presence of peace. Perhaps there is no better scripture that pictures the daily state of mind that a believer should be in than today's passage. "This is the day which the Lord hath made; we will rejoice and be glad in it!" Today is a day that was made by God. In fact there has only been seven total days that were ever made. All of the other days are repeats of the initial and original days. Mondays will always be Mondays; just like Fridays will always be Fridays until the end of time. So every day is a day to be glad. No matter how we feel, no matter what's going wrong, no matter what we are facing; it's still a day that the Lord has made – rejoice and be glad in it! For those who don't know why we should be glad; there are millions of reasons. First of all, He woke us up this morning! Thank God for letting you see today. It could have been the other way. Somebody laid down last night but didn't get back up. They slept all night; but couldn't rise this morning. But God has given us another day to live; be glad. Secondly, we know who we are. The elders within my community used to say; "I was clothed in my right mind." If you know who you are, you should be thankful. Somebody has a mind but it doesn't work right. They are confused on who they are and what life is all about. But you and I know who we are and we know who should get the praise. We should be glad because we can think of His goodness through this day, look back over our lives, and remember how good He has been – be glad. Finally, we have a right to be glad. It's amazing that all kinds of groups are proud of what they stand for. They come out and celebrate their organization and their goals for the future. It's time for us to be glad and tell somebody. Stop walking around with your head hanging down. Rise up and be glad in the Lord. Give Him the praise.

Day 80

Be Planted

> Psalms 1:3 And he shall be like a tree planted
> by the rivers of water, that bringeth forth his
> fruit in his season; his leaf also shall not wither;
> and whatsoever he doeth shall prosper.

When something is planted it is deliberately placed somewhere to flourish and thrive. One of the very first commandments that God gave to mankind was to "be fruitful and multiply." There are four basic operations in arithmetic: addition, subtraction, division, and multiplication. To multiply is to increase in numbers by multitudes. Obviously multitudes are defined as great numbers that exist in multiples and multiplication is increasing numbers at an increasing rate. Unlike addition that increases numbers too; multiplication simplifies addition by doubling, tripling, and in many cases significantly increasing the total number (increasing at an increased rate). God places fruitfulness and multiplication together in many scriptures. In other words, to be fruitful is to increase at an increasing rate. Each believer has to be planted to be productive. There is simply no way to be fruitful without being planted in God. We can never manifest what we possess until we first become rooted in the Lord. As children of God we should be manifesting externally what we possess internally. Somebody ought to be able to see spiritual fruit on our trees. They should not only be able to see fruit, but much fruit. They should be able to see fruit that is increasing at an increasing rate; i.e. (fruit, more fruit, much fruit)! Yes it is the will of God for us to increase physically, emotionally, and spiritually continually. The fruit on our trees are the sure signs of maturity and development. It needs to be understood that the process will take time. God can do things instantly; but God isn't going to put fruit on an unplanted tree. Neither is He going to put a lot fruit on a tree that is incapable of handling the fruit. A two feet tree could never support twenty fruit! What branch can Christ add fruit to in your life? Where is the most growth? The Bible teaches that faith comes by hearing and hearing by the Word of God. An increase in faith will eventually led to an increase in fruit. Before we start trying to receive our harvest, we need to have something on the tree. And there will never be anything on the tree if we remain unplanted. We simply have too many unplanted people in church today; unplanted preachers who aren't preaching the gospel, unplanted leaders who are inconsistent in leadership, and unplanted members who are unstable as water. There are two kinds of unplanted people: 1) those who have never been planted, 2) those who were once planted but have been plucked up! It's time for us to get planted and produce fruit.

Day 81

Be Prosperous

> Psalms 1:3 And he shall be like a tree planted by the rivers of water, that bringeth forth his fruit in his season; his leaf also shall not wither; and whatsoever he doeth shall prosper.

Prosperity is certainly a part of the Christian life. The Apostle John wrote that he wished above all things that we would prosper and be in health, even as our souls prosper. The prosperity of the soul has been interpreted to be the continued spiritual development of a person's life. God wants us to prosper. The life of a Christian is one that should be filled with blessings of all kinds. Blessings should be running after us, chasing us down and meeting us in places that we never suspected. In the passage, the Psalmist is talking about the lifestyle of a person who is blessed. He or she will be like a tree planted by the rivers of water. A tree that is planted by water will never become dried out. The idea of being placed in the right location to prosper has merit. So many times we want to be blessed but we aren't planted near the water. We can't expect to produce fruit if we're planted in dry places. Indeed, victory comes to those who are near the water. When trees and plants don't receive an adequate amount of water their leaves will eventually begin to wither. Withering is a sign that someone or something isn't getting what they need.

Unfortunately, there are times when we simply aren't getting what we need. It can happen in relationships, churches, careers, and even from your family. Not getting what we need creates within itself a deficiency. Yet the Bible teaches us that a blessed person will not only get what they need; but also will prosper. It is the will of God for us to move forward and increase. Good things happen when we are planted in the right place and receiving everything that we need to grow and be fruitful. Nothing in this world can satisfy us like God can and He wants us to be prosperous. Prosperity is not just about money and finances; but it's about the entirety of a person's life. It's the fullness of existence and the complete makeup of our life's order. Prosperity has more to do with the "way" in which we live versus the things that we possess. Too often preachers only speak about prosperity in light of possessions instead of teaching about the position. When we get into position (planted by the water) prosperity isn't as difficult as we think it would be. In fact prosperity can happen for us right now. We don't have to do something spectacular or perform a remarkable feat to receive it; all we need to do is get into position. The Psalmist informs us that if we get into position – "whatever" we do will prosper! This is a tremendous promise to God's people. Where we are planted determines what we receive.

Day 82

Be of Good Courage

> Psalms 27:14 Wait on the Lord: be of
> good courage, and he shall strengthen
> thine heart: wait, I say, on the Lord.

Courage is the lack of fear when facing troubling and dangerous situations. It takes courage to stand up against the odds and do what is right, especially when all tendencies are leading toward what is wrong. Throughout Biblical history, numerous people have displayed great courage when facing difficult circumstances. It took courage for Moses just to go back to Egypt but much more courage to present himself to Pharaoh and make an unbelievable request. He had fled from Egypt as a criminal and was likely remembered as a murderer who never served his time for the crime. He was also exposed as a Hebrew that was raised in Pharaoh's court and could have easily been killed for false impersonation. There were numerous charges that could have been brought against him for fleeing the scene of a crime and covering up what he did. Yet God sent him back to the very people who were seeking his life – that took courage. It also took courage for David to face Goliath with nothing but a slingshot. Goliath was the champion of the Philistines and he was very well equipped to fight. There is no record of how many soldiers that Goliath had already killed prior to David; but there's little doubt that he was far more experienced in battle than David. In fact, David had never actually been in a battle at all and was very content with watching the battle from a safe demilitarized zone. But when he saw how Goliath defied the living God, something arose in David. David was filled with courage and brought a giant down to the ground. It took courage for Joshua to march around the walls of Jericho for seven days. Out of all the conventional warfare tactics known to mankind, no one had ever utilized such an incomprehensible approach to winning a battle. Marching around an impenetrable wall with the army following behind a group of musicians and worshippers is not a normal way to win. Joshua's courage proved to be faithful because God gave them the city. When they shouted, the walls fell down flat and they conquered Jericho with the might of God Himself. It took major courage for Abraham to leave his family and journey to a land unknown to him. So much attention is focused on His faith until very little it placed on how courageous he had to be to obey God. Not many people who are already established would venture beyond their comfort zones to places unknown; but Abraham did. God is looking for courageous people. The Psalmist writes: "wait on the Lord, and be of good courage!" In other words, waiting on God requires courage. He may not come when you want Him to come, but He's always on time.

Day 83

Be Made Whole

John 5:6 When Jesus saw him lie, and knew that he had been now a long time in that case, he saith unto him, Wilt thou be made whole?

Being made whole is what life in Christ is all about. So often people come to Jesus, but never fully realize that salvation is more than an "event" but it's also an "evolution." Christ has come to bring us from where we were to take us where we should be. The transformative power of Christ continually changes us from old to new and from then to now. In essence, being whole is being made into the fullness of the content. When something is full, it can no longer hold any more. Fullness is all of the capacity of being full. In other words the whole thing is intact. When we are not whole, we are broken, fractured, divided, incomplete, and partial. Yes, a believer can be incomplete in all kinds of areas in their lives. And when we are incomplete, we tend to give incomplete service. It's hard to give 100% when your heart is divided. Fractured believers give fractured praise and worship. It's time out for only 1/3 of our commitment and consistency. God deserves our best. Just as anything else has challenges; so does being whole. The process of making a person whole involves putting them together one piece at a time. It starts with W-Willingness. If we are willing we can change. No one will ever change if they are constantly blaming their shortcomings on others. Willingness has to do with yielding your will to His and saying: "yes" to change. The next letter is H-Humility. Being humble is the key to growth. Too often, gifted and talented people lack the humility needed to sustain their blessings. We all need to take doses of humility daily. Following Humility is O-Openness. Most believers don't mind saying that they are open to the Lord, but they aren't open to His correction. If we can ever be made whole there has to be openness to His Spirit in all areas of our lives. Following Openness is L-Listening. When we can hear, we can do. We can't hear without an ear and the ear is not physical but spiritual. The final part is E-Eagerness. We can attain eagerness from all kinds of ways. Inspiration can come from some of the most unlikely places. Yet the birthing of consistent eagerness has to be embedded within one's own personal passion and motivation. These are the real ways to be made whole. All other methods will only lead to temporary changes and more frustration.

Day 84

Dealing with Disappointment

> Proverbs 13:12 Hope deferred maketh the heart sick: but when the desire cometh, it is a tree of life.

No one can live this life without having to deal with disappointments. People will disappoint us, and sometimes we can disappoint ourselves by our very own actions. Is your life like you thought it would be at this stage of your journey? It's very likely that you expected to be closer to your goals than you are. Well, you are not alone. Statistics confirm that most people have an optimistic view of life while planning their future, but fail to include the pitfalls and setbacks. While it only takes four years to complete a bachelor's degree (for most majors), in reality many people need more than four. It's also possible to get hired for your dream job fresh out of college, but it's not likely. It's a slight chance that you'll become famous, rich, or even powerful one day; but the likelihood is slim to none. There is a phenomenon called "15 minutes of fame." The phrase was coined back in 1968, but with modern media, you-tube, and all kinds of social outlets; it's easy to become a sensation overnight. However, people who look to become famous, rich, or powerful quickly will only enjoy a brief and short-lived celebrity status. Why? Because there will always be a new search for the next best thing. The passage points out that disappointments abound in every arena of life. When hopes are dashed against the walls of reality; we are forced to face the facts; and sometimes facing the facts isn't an enjoyable experience. Therefore we must learn how to appropriately deal with disappointments. First of all we must 1) Keep our faith in God. Believe it or not, lots of believers are disappointed with God. No, they aren't brave enough to say it; but their lives reflect it. It's hard to pray to God if you feel or think He isn't listening or doesn't care. So in order to deal with disappointment we must keep our faith in God no matter what. Secondly we must 2) Keep our priorities straight. It's easy to lose your way when things aren't working out as you thought. Yes, that happens to believers too. We can lose our way and get off track when what we wanted or desired has not materialized. It's important to prioritize and focus on what actually matters. Sometimes that means going back to the very basics of necessity. Thirdly we must 3) Keep our timetables open. To everything there is season and a time. We must remain open to the possibility of change. It is very possible that God may not come when we want Him too nor do things in the way that we prefer. He knows what's best for our future even if it looks like it's hurting us in the present. We can't avoid disappointments; but we can learn from them and move on.

Day 85

Dealing with Frustration

Psalms 43:5 Why art thou cast down, O my soul? and why art thou disquieted within me? hope in God: for I shall yet praise him, who is the health of my countenance, and my God.

Have you ever been frustrated? I mean really, really, really frustrated? I've been preaching the Gospel for many years and I've seen first-hand how Christians don't like to talk about their feelings. It's almost as if we have to disconnect our minds and become emotionally detached from ourselves to be saved. Yet the Bible is filled with people of God who showed their frustrations with life. Of course we should not be known for having gloom gatherings and pity parties every time something doesn't go our way but we do have the liberty to express how we feel. God knows our hearts anyway. Frustration is defined as a common emotional response to opposition. It's directly linked to disappointments that are a result of a person's will (desires, wishes, and goals) being constantly resisted. The greater the obstruction and resistance exist, the greater the frustration will persists. There are internal and external factors that usually contribute to our frustrations. Sometimes we can be frustrated with the way we internally handle issues. Whenever certain buttons are pushed we are more or less likely to respond in a particular way. Obviously, external factors play a large part of personal frustrations too. The external factors are mostly all outside of our control. We each have things that we wish could be changed immediately. Yet in reality we don't possess the power to fix everything in life exactly like we want it to be. So how do we deal with frustration? I believe that this passage gives us some important pieces to the process. In Psalms 43, the Psalmist is frustrated. He asks God to judge him and make a ruling in his favor. Ungodly people that seem to have the upper hand surround the writer. He also seems to be uncertain about which way to go next with his life and what is happening "to him" externally is affecting him internally. But he does three intentional acts that lifted him above his frustrations: 1) He said I will go to the altar of God. In spite of what he's going through, he keeps church attendance as a major part of his life. 2) He personally praises God. He said: "with the harp I will praise my God." We should never depend on someone else to praise God for us when we can do it ourselves. 3) He keeps his faith and hope intact. He never loses hope regardless to how frustrated things are to him. You may be one of the many people reading this devotional who have become frustrated with specific things in your life. Whatever may be frustrating you isn't going to win. Take courage and look up but remain intentional in your actions.

Day 86

Dealing with Setbacks

Joshua 7:4 So there went up thither of the people about three thousand men: and they fled before the men of Ai.

A setback is an unanticipated or sudden change in progress from better to worse. In some cases a setback is a reversal of fortune that may even include a defeat. We all have setbacks in this life and we don't have to live long to experience the challenges associated with them. A songwriter wrote a song that said: "time is filled with swift transitions." It is often in the "swift transitions" of day-to-day activity that we encounter a few setbacks. Good people experience setbacks. Churches experience setbacks too. I've known of many churches and denominations that were once thriving and striving; but changes in the times left them behind. Unfortunately, some churches have been set back so far until they have become completely irrelevant to their community. There's little life, no youth, and very few converts being brought forth in their congregations. Marriages can experience setbacks. Many couples begin their journey together while floating on cloud nine, but troubles and trials reduces them to ground zero and they are struggling to stay together. The idea of being setback is not one that we desire to happen to us; yet in reality, we have to deal with them. Two steps forward and three steps backwards is a net gain of negative one. In other words, setbacks move us backwards instead of propelling us forward. So many believers are living their spiritual lives with "net" negative progress. They aren't moving forward at all. Sure we will have setbacks; but with God, those setbacks can be turned into comebacks. This is what happens in the story of Joshua concerning the little town called Ai. Ai should have been the easiest victory in the campaign to take over the Promised Land, but it turned into a living nightmare. When easy things become hard; something is wrong. I once talked with somebody about his talents. This person was very gifted and used his talent with such ease until he made it look simple. He could flow, deliver, and finish strong as he operated within his calling; but one day, he started struggling to do it. Almost overnight and without warning he was no longer able to do what he had done for many years. We spoke about what happened and he shared that there were some issues that he had been dealing with behind the scenes. He had unresolved matters that had finally took a toll of his ability – sin was in his life. The same thing happened in the battle of Ai. Sin was in the camp and God couldn't bless the people. But when Joshua addressed the matter directly and purged the camp of its sin, the setback became a setup for a comeback.

Day 87

Dealing with Mistakes

Job 19:4 And be it indeed that I have erred,
mine error remaineth with myself.

A mistake is an error in action, calculation, opinion, or judgment caused by poor reasoning, carelessness, and insufficient knowledge. I was in a conference once and the facilitator said something that was interesting. He said "every manager is entitled to one huge, enormous, gigantic, mind-blowing, inexcusable mistake; but anything after that brings your competence into question." In other words; too many mistakes is a reflection of your character and ability to perform the requirements. I'm thankful that God doesn't have us living on a "one mistake" policy. If He did, none of us would ever stay on the job long enough to get anything done. As long as we are human, there is within every one of us the capacity to make mistakes. We can make mistakes very easily and quickly and be totally unaware of the error. If you've ever had to write a paper for class, I'm sure you also proofread it and corrected your spelling and grammar before you turned it in. Did it come back from your instructor, after being graded, with mistakes? How many typos were in your last formal communication or email? Unfortunately, for some people, one of the hardest things to do is to admit that they make mistakes. I believe that part of the resistance has to do with the "perceived" idea that once we are saved we are also flawless. There's probably nothing more farther from the truth that this awful misconception. And as long as we live we will continue to make mistakes. When it comes to people, we can make character judgment mistakes, when it comes to life, we can make mistakes in our decisions, and when it comes to finances, we can make mistakes all too often. How do we deal with mistakes: 1) Admit them. The first step to deliverance is always admittance. Don't be afraid to admit it when you've made an error. And learn to stop being afraid of being pointed out and called out for making mistakes; because the people who are judging you are making mistakes too. Maybe their mistakes are not in the same area of yours or in the same manner of yours but they have flaws too. 2) Correct them. If you've caused someone to stumble and miss the mark with your mistake, correct it. Don't expect things to just autocorrect. A contractor once told me, "if I'm off by an inch on the foundation; I'll be off by a yard on the roof." 3) Avoid or reduce them. We can avoid and reduce making mistakes by being more cautious and deliberate in our efforts. Obviously, if we're talking about things that don't have eternal significance or life-altering affects, making mistakes isn't as impacting. But when it comes to your destiny, salvation, and spiritual growth; the fewer mistakes we make; the better off we will be in the long run.

Day 88

Perfect in Weakness

2 Corinthians 12:9 And he said unto me, My grace is sufficient for thee: for my strength is made perfect in weakness.

An antonym is a term used to describe words that have an opposite meaning. Antonyms are different from synonyms because synonyms describe words that are the same or are very similar. Antonyms use polarizing and differing terms of words and their meanings and capture the full extreme of each side. All of us have used antonyms at some point or another in our lifetime. In fact we use them or have an understanding knowledge of them without even trying to think that much about it. And while we strive to find things that work well together, look for ways to bring unity, and work at how we can resolve our differences; there is the real reality that opposites (antonyms) play a major part in things that we deal with daily. Perhaps there is no other Bible verse that embodies an antonym than this passage. The opposite of strength is weakness. These two words are extremely different. They are so different until it is virtually impossible to confuse when something is strong verse something that is weak. When we think about things that are weak, other words tend to come to mind too; like frail, fragile, and unstable. But as we consider the word "strong" we can't help but think about brute, vitality, and stability. In most cases, when given a choice, I venture to say that the majority of us would rather be strong than weak. We would prefer a position of strength as opposed to that of weakness when dealing with finances. Of course if the banker or creditor told you that you have a "strong" financial portfolio; those words would bring much peace to your mind. If the doctor examined your heart and said you have a strong heart that's full of vitality; you would be more assured rather than if he stated your heart was weak and failing. Yet in the passage, God tells the Apostle Paul that His strength is made perfect in Paul's weakness. The background of the text informs us that Paul was dealing with a "thorn in his side." He finds out much later that the thorn was actually a messenger of Satan that was sent to buffet (resist and withstand) him. Paul prayed earnestly about this thorn for three definitive times and God eventually answered him with a strong exhortation. God said – "My grace is sufficient for you." Praise God! No matter what the devil has permission to attack us with or use in his plan against us; God's grace is enough to handle it. Somebody may be feeling that you're just too weak to keep fighting this battle that you're in. It may even seem like it's costing you too much mental capital to hang in there; but don't give up now. You're weakest moment is only an antonym for what God is about to perform in your life. When we are weak, He is strong.

Day 89

A Life in Progress

> Ecclesiastes 2:24 There is nothing better for a man, than that he should eat and drink, and that he should make his soul enjoy good in his labour. This also I saw, that it was from the hand of God.

Someone once said: "we can be so busy trying to make a living until we never get a chance to live." I've seen people work hard to get to the point of retirement and actually retire with expectations of living the remainder of their lives in pleasure. Unfortunately, some of them didn't live long enough to enjoy the many years of Social Security and pensions that they'd built up. For years they had worked very hard and dedicated their whole lives to advancement. They worked themselves up from their bootstraps to make it. Some of them were single parents, others were factory workers, many were military enlisted; but their goals were very similar – do better. Isn't that why we work hard every day? We want to make a better live for our families and especially our children. There are a few things that we shouldn't forget while we're at work. First of all, let's not forget that we should enjoy working. Anyone who goes to work every day and hates it will have a hard time. Work is supposed to be fulfilling and rewarding. If you are miserable on your job, you have to ask yourself a few pointed questions. Is this the right career path for me? Can

I see myself doing this for the next five to ten years? Secondly, we should function as a believer at work. Whatever we do in our places of employment should be an extension of what we do at church. In other words, we should not be one way at church and another way on the job. Thirdly, work should be a place for opportunity and growth. If you're in a place where there is no way for you to advance beyond the point where you are; pray and think about it again. Of course I'm not telling you to quit your job today and leave; but I'm encouraging you to pray and think clearly about your future. God expects us to enjoy the fruit of our labor. Yes, I believe that we should be able to get things that we desire if we've worked for them but I'm also apprehensive about getting everything that we want. Usually something happens when we start getting everything that we want – we tend to stray away from God. I know some good people who started out faithful to their church; but the "cares of this world," "the lust of other things," and the "pride of life," had them so far into debt until they had no choice but to work on Sundays and any other available time. Your life is already in progress; be smart enough to recognize it. Yes, you need to do what you have to do; but don't forget to do what you "need" to do too. Give God some of your time and never give a place of employment more of your commitment than you do to Christ.

Day 90

Good Things Are Coming!

> Psalms 125:4 Do good, O Lord, unto those that be good, and to them that are upright in their hearts.

Most of us are familiar with the saying: "good things come to those who wait." The sense and meaning of this saying is actually a word of encouragement to someone who desires and is wishing for change. Opportunities are present and decisions need to be made; but they are waiting for something better. Yes, life is filled with all kinds of opportunities and open doors. Yet all open doors are not of the Lord. A spiritually mature person usually is able to recognize what is of God and what is not. However, there are times when the lines are blurry and the opportunities may look promising, but it is still not of God. We must be very cautious in decisions making, especially when it comes to major decisions that will have a lasting impact. God is good! Perhaps there is no better adjective that describes the nature and personality of God than that of being good. We serve a good God. He's so good until His very nature (what makes Him who He is) pours goodness. The passage points out that God does good things to those whose are good and to those whose heart is in tune with His heart. Just like we can fine tune and instrument such as a piano, guitar, saxophone, and all others; to play the best sound; and just like we can tune our radios and televisions to receive the maximum signal, so can we tune our hearts to our God. When we are out of tune, our hearts cannot sense, feel, recognize, or even be conscious of what God is actually trying to do. I see people all the time who totally miss what God is doing. What's even more disappointing is the fact that they are incapable of recognizing His movement because it can only happen in the heart. But good things come to those who are good and whose heart is in tune with Him! If you know you've been doing good and living in the light; take courage because good things are coming to you. Don't be depressed and live in fear anymore; the breakthrough is here. Rise up and accept what the Lord is getting ready to do. Good things are coming to you! Good things are coming to you! Good things are coming to you! You don't have to settle for less than the best out of life. Be patient and be ready because when you least expect something to come, it's closer than you thought. Don't give up in the middle of your breakthrough! You've come too far to turn around now. We are claiming every promise of God! This will be a new beginning for you and good things coming right now! Receive it in Jesus Holy name!

CPSIA information can be obtained
at www.ICGtesting.com
Printed in the USA
FFHW011249220719
53813256-59488FF